$\mathcal{THE}$ $\mathcal{BRIDGE}$ 2

$\mathcal{REVISED}$

Preface

So many textbooks seek to take high school level English students and move forward without bridging the gap between the expectations of pre-college and college-level writing. This is a textbook designed for a generation of writers that have been raised in different cultures and on a range of technologies – inspired by books, media and video games – and versed in traditional and non-traditional study patterns. It is also a book for writers from other language backgrounds because when students get to a certain level, a lot of the writing issues converge to cross cultural and linguistic backgrounds.

After you realize that you can write essays and that they are indeed not that hard, you can become a "composition machine." That is someone who understands the importance of structure and dares to research and prove their ideas are valid and interesting. If you follow these teachings and complete the assignments step-by-step, your writing **will** improve. Not only that, but you'll begin to feel confident about your ability to express academic thoughts. Never underestimate the power of confidence in your abilities. You won't just be right because you think you're right. After learning composition skills, you will be right because you know how to prove that your point of view is valid. Now this might not sound that useful sitting around the dinner table winning arguments with your brother or family, but learning to push forward a good idea at work or in school can lead to big things. That is the goal of this book: to unlock your ideas and present them in the best way possible.

Now if you are feeling like you haven't written in a while, don't worry, you'll be writing soon. If you feel your skills aren't ready for this level, you're probably wrong. Most of the people who doubt their work also have the study tools necessary to bring their abilities in line with expectation. Finally, if you feel like writing is a tedious process that only a few people can execute properly, get ready to have your world rocked. Writing is about you and unless you're bored with you (I see you sitting back in the back with the baseball cap) this class should move you into a more confident state of mind in every class in which you choose to participate.

Have Fun, Write Lots, and Work Hard
The Authors

TABLE OF CONTENTS

THE BRIDGE 2 - PART I

THE BRIDGE 2 - PART II
THE WRITING MODULES

CHAPTER ONE
Journals

What is it about writing that makes it so difficult to sit down and do? Is it the cursor blinking, mocking the word processing student? Is it the paper? The lines are so straight and uniform. We need to get past the idea that writing is a chore and journals are the way to do it. Journals are one of the first forms of writing dating back to the days of Marcus Aurelius, but don't just take the Romans' word for it. Journaling can be a great way to break the barrier between the fearful scribe and the confident one.

Many students do not actually enjoy journal writing, but perhaps it is all in the perspective. In order to improve your writing, you need to write and you need to write frequently. That is how you improve. That is how you make writing a part of your life and your academic routine. Journals give you the opportunity to write regularly throughout the course while completing exercises from the book and essay assignments. Sometimes these things will overlap and that is a beneficial thing as you are able to apply one area to another and you are able to reflect on work done and being done. It is through self-reflection that great learning strides can be made.

Student Example Journal - Description

A time that I felt I was in serious danger but ended up being fine, was a time when I was living in Santa Barbara and there was a huge fire within a mile from my house. When I went to bed that night I knew there was a small fire but I did not think it was going to get worse and end up getting out of hand. It was 1:30 am when I got woken up to the phone ringing. One of my friends had called me and asked if I had evacuated from my house yet. I was not aware of how serious this fire got and that I was in serious danger. I yelled for my mom and dad and got no response. I was so worried, what do I do, where did they go? I was all alone. I called my dad on his cell phone, he answered immediately asking, "are you ok?" At that point I had been crying and almost couldn't get out my words. Where are you? I said. Him and my mom had to go to the barn a couple miles from my house to evacuate our horses. But he told me he was about to leave and come back home while my mom stayed and finished getting all the barn stuff together and situated. When I got off the phone with him I immediately turned on my TV to get information about the fire. Soon after I heard the door bell ring. It was a police officer telling me we need to evacuate ASAP. I was home alone and started to freak out. Thankfully my dad had made it home shortly after and helped me get all of our valuables together and packed into the car. As we exited our street you could see the fire burning down the house at the end of our street. I was so scared for my life and for our house. In the end every thing ended our house and all of us ended up surviving and being just fine.

The English is not perfect, but the idea is conveyed in a way that is very personal and descriptive and that is an important part of the writing process. Journals are a way to share experience through text and therefore aren't usually as strict or as structured as paragraph and essay assignments in a composition class. Even the reflection journal below which is more traditionally academic in content still maintains the personal tone.

Student Example Journal – Reflection

Hard work is the key to success in college. First, as a college student I need to keep in mind the fact that I have responsibilities myself. This is a very important point if I want to be a successful student. My obligations are to attend to class on time, participate in class, and do the homework that is assigned in class on time. These are all my responsibilities; no one else can help me. Also, it is necessary to learn the importance of time management. Not doing this would make me fall behind really quickly. If a class is missed, I will have no idea of what the teacher is talking about the next day. If I do not find time to do the homework, I will lose points. Arriving late to class will disturb my fellow colleagues and it is disrespectful. Also, I can be dropped from the class for continued lateness. On the other hand, getting everything done at the right time, doing my part, and working hard will lead me to achieve my goals. Sometimes it is really easy to leave all the responsibility to the teacher or the instructor. Some people think that having a good instructor is the key to success in college, but I disagree with this statement. It is true that a good instructor could be really helpful and will make my way easy; but it is not the instructor's responsibility to make me a successful student. I can still be successful without a good instructor if I use the other resources available to all of us such as the tutoring learning center, computer lab, the library, peers, friends, family and maybe other instructors. Also, I can ask the teacher questions for clarification, and it may help me and my peers understand the class better. Participating in a study group outside the class is also a good idea, and if there is no group created, I can always star a new one. As you can see, there are different things I can do to help myself. It will be my decision to work hard and make everything work out or to sit down on my chair and blame my instructor for my failure in college. If I work hard during my college years a world of opportunities will be waiting for me out there and I will do my best effort to accomplish all my goals and achieve my dreams.

The final example below is in response to a specific prompt on behavior. The student responds with a short journal about her father and then three other students provide short feedback for the student.

Student Example Journal and Responses
While I started to think about the people's different behaviors that I have observed around me, I realized that the only behavior that I have a high regard for is my Dad's

courage. He proved that two years ago by deciding to leave everything he obtained in order to take his children to a better place. My dad was a successful constructor and he used to work really hard for his family so that they do not to have a hard time. Since he was a teenager he used to help his father with the job and as the older son of family he felt responsible for his younger brother and sisters. Although he was having a hard time taking all that responsibility himself, he succeeded in his job. He ran his own company and had worked for almost 25 years in this condition. By the time he realized that his children might not have a stable future in Iran he decided to take us to better place so that we can study and have a new life. He left all that experience and that successful job just because of us. Although he knew that starting a new life in a new country with different language is hard enough to make him unhappy he did it for us! I admire his courage and his self-giving .I know that he might not like living here, or to being here with all those language difficulties and I am just thinking about things that would make him happy. I have promised myself that I will be the best daughter for him. I will graduate from the best university so that he would be proud of me. I want to show him that what he did for us meant so much to me. If I happen to be very successful in my life, that is because of my admirable father.

Hi Samantha

This is Azadi. I like the way you are talking about your father, when I was read your journal I just remember my father. It is so hard for him to left behind all his successful position and his company and challenging with new language and maybe new job here, but I am sure he is so happy because he could do something that he felt righ for you. Definitely you disserve to graduate from one of the best university and of course, you are the best daughter for him even if you never graduated from the good university.

Hi Samantha,
   I am so touched with your story. From time to time I think about my family in this sense. Mostly my father because he is the breadwinner in my family. He is also a hard working man and he is trying his best to support me for a better future. I admire him a lot. Some people want to be rich, or famous , i just want to be like my father. Being a good father and to have a family as mine is my wish. That is why i am here and working hard, so one day i can be like my father in the future. I just want to be able to support a happy and great life for my family. Especially my future kids, if i can support a good life as my father did to me, then i will consider myself successful in life.

Samantha, I am touched with your great story and I think that people who's closer gives influence to others. I think that some fathers will do anything for their family to be happy. It's good that your father is giving to good influence because you learn many things from him. Your journal sounds great to me and even though your dad is struggling, I believe that he's happy because your healthy and your happy. Some people don't really have a father just like your father, so know that your gifted and he's also gifted. I believe that he will get through with things that are struggling him and your going to be great daughter. Keep it up with your work.

The goal of a journal is to take an assigned topic and write in a way that conveys your ideas on the topic. If a journal assignment is descriptive, it should involve the senses. A teacher wants to hear, smell, see and feel your trip to the Grand Canyon much more than he wants to know about the gas mileage that you got on the way to the Grand Canyon. The first is a personal account the other is an objective (although each car will be different I grant) reality. In a composition class, you need to be able to write in both styles. If the journal assignment is reflective, it should involve exactly that reflection on what you did but also analysis. Like the descriptive assignment, this one is personal as it is you reflecting on your progress, your behavior, your perceptions and so forth.

Should we have our first assignment already? We should.

EMAIL OR WEB SPECIAL - Journals

This is an assignment that is designed to span ten weeks. Your instructor can set you up to post these journals on the web, on a discussion board or have them relayed to two other students in the form of email. The mode of delivery is NOT as important as the commitment to writing 300 words a week for the next ten weeks.

Be sure to label each one of them numerically (Journal One, Journal Two and so forth).

You are required to follow and comment on the journals of two other students. A comment is 150 words minimum. To receive full credit, you must comment on all of the journals of two other students (that is twenty comments minimum).

Your journals may be part of your grade (ask your professor) and in this format are essentially blogs. To do the journals successfully, you need to do the following:

1. Follow the rules for the journals.
2. Meet the 300 word minimum.
3. Submit the journals on time.
4. Follow and comment on two other students' journals.

Journal Assignments

Journal 1
Write your thoughts on modern day diaries such as Facebook and other social

networking sites. Use ideas from your class discussions.

Journal 2
Interview a family member about the cover story in the LA or NY Times. Use quotes from your family member in the journal to indicate their actual words on the topic.

Journal 3
Describe a behavior you observed and admired.

Journal 4
What do you believe the most important things about learning and how you learn are? How does what you believe affect your behavior?
Journal 5
Go to youtube.com find a video and comment on it.

Journal 6
Your first essay. Your process, your challenges, your grade, your expectations, your goals for future essays.

Journal 7
Call a local college or University and ask them about the process of applying to be a student. Ask them if there are any tips for submitting the perfect application. Write the process that they relay in your journal.

Journal 8
If you are reading a book in class, discuss your favorite character. If you are not reading a book in class, discuss your favorite character from a movie or TV.

Journal 9
The joys and frustrations of researching and writing essays.

Journal 10
A favorite song or poem copy, paste, explain what it means to you.

IN-CLASS ACTIVITY
Get into a group of three. Discuss the following:

Why do people write a diary?
If you found the diary of a friend would you read it?
Do you think that Facebook status counts as a modern diary? What are some things you would never put on your Facebook or social networking account?

Make notes below.

_____

_____

_____

_____

_____

Report your ideas to the class and challenge them to question you. Learn from the questions your peers ask. Are there any questions posed in the reporting that you should have considered in the discussion time?

_____

_____

_____

React to this quote:

"Twitter condenses and therefore ruins written communication for anyone who has thoughts of greater complexity than 140 characters." English Major

_____

_____

_____

_____

_____

_____

_____

Share your reactions in groups. Did you have similar responses?

CHAPTER TWO PRE-WRITING

While journals are a form of regular writing, pre-writing is a more focused technique to generate ideas for, in this case, academic assignments. Many textb ooks spend much time on this aspect of writing, this textbook will dedicate some time as it is important. We also recognize that prewriting is personal and students have their own way of "getting started." That being said, students are often stuck in a particular way of writing or generating ideas which may make them hesitant to try new methods. Alternatively, some students simply have no way of beginning and need to be introduced to new methods in order to find the one that works best for them. Now you can see why we and you need to address pre-writing!

You may think that things will arrange themselves in a coherent manner at some point but it really is important to organize your thoughts from the very beginning. We will use brainstorming in complete sentences and clustering to make the concept of how to start a paper more clear and attainable. We will begin with something very accessible and move to topics that are complex and academic, so don't roll your eyes when you get the first topic.

Ways to get to school

Every paper feels the same way when it is first presented as an assignment: impossible. What's interesting about that? What am I supposed to write? How can I write about this for two weeks of my life and be any the better for it? Well, calm those thoughts for now although they may serve you well in later, more artistic pursuits.

Start by putting your pen on a blank piece of paper, or your fingers on the keys and write complete sentences that relate in your mind to "ways to get to school."

Write ten sentences below (or on the computer):

1.

2.

3.

4.

5.

6.

7.

8.

9.

10.

Groups

Now look at the sentences you have written. Read some of them to your group and make sure you mention the number each time you read one. Do you notice any pattern? Have your group members choose the best ones. Where did the best ones come on the brainstorming list?

Usually the best ideas come after your first three choices. Why might that be? I tell my students to throw out the first three ideas and make a paper out of the rest. This is important because so many students sit down to write and only go as far as their first three ideas. Often these ideas are unbalanced, obvious and or just not that interesting. Number 10 really took some thought so it is either trivial or fantastic. Either way, it is nice to know you can get to ten. It shows versatility and growth. Pat yourself on the back. Pat your colleague on the back.

Did you also notice how having another pair of eyes look over your work helps you? The importance of peers and feedback in writing is not to be underestimated. We need each other and we need each other at every stage of the writing process.

Pre-Writing Clustering

Now that we have some good ideas, let's start looking at them in a different way. Let's also kick it up a bit and make the topic more academic in nature. Instead of "Ways to get to school"

Ways to get into Harvard

Notice that it is the same topic, but when it is narrowed this way, we can actually research and develop a plan or model that will help a student with the goal of getting into Harvard. This broadens the topic from the original one, which really might only be valuable to someone who lives in your neighborhood or lives the same distance from your school. It is interesting the way a simple modification can take a topic and put it into a more academic light. The first thing you do when clustering is find a central idea and put it into the hub of your diagram. Look below.

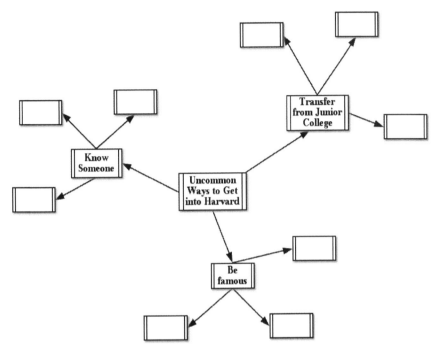

EMAIL OR WEB SPECIAL

Now it's time to fill in the boxes. Go to your favorite search engine and fill in the empty rectangles with examples of students who got into Harvard in these uncommon ways. Find people who were famous before they went to Harvard. Find people who knew members of the staff or faculty before attending and find stories of students who transferred from a Jr. College (yes, that is possible). Notice that clustering not only makes you research a topic, but it also forces your mind to connect each point to the topic. Imagine drawing an arrow from Uncommon Ways to get into Harvard to a story about getting into Yale. You could actually visualize the mistake and correct it in the planning process.

Share your research with your peers in the next class. Later we will make rules about what research is proper for a college essay and what is not, but for now just look everywhere you can.

Chapter Two Writing Assignment

This first assignment bridges the gap between a journal and an essay; it is a narrative paragraph assignment.

Tell a story that spans less than a month of your life.

Don't write about your entire childhood or even a year of your life. Narrow it down to a story about a particular part of your life. Use description like you would support in an essay. This means that you should pay attention to details of action, sight, smell, and feeling in narrative writing; don't just say "I went to Washington." Describe the experience in full.

This writing should be at least 450 words in length. When you bring it to class you will be asked to get into groups based on the topic of the writing. You will have to discuss your stories briefly and decide which stories belong together and why. You will not have a formal presentation of your story, but you will hand it in after deciding to which group it belongs.

Writing Break I
Terminology

Your instructor will inevitably be using the language of composition throughout the course. These terms are important to the study of writing and to the shaping of your own writing. It is essential to know what they mean – and also have a discussion about what they mean together. This gives you a common language for the class and for the rest of the course.

Write your own definitions for each term then compare them with other students' responses.

Example from class:

Student: *Support means items used to get the reader to believe what you are saying.*

Instructor: *I think you have to be careful about how you define support. Support really should be expert testimony. This can come in the form of statistics, quotes, analysis, but it should always come from a respected authority in the field of study.*

- Introduction

- Body Paragraph

- Conclusion

- Thesis Statement

- Unity

- Coherence

- Voice

- Content

- Support

- Plagiarism

- Peer

- Cause/Effect

- Comparison

- Contrast

- Argumentation

- Classification

Are there any other terms that you have come across? Ask your instructor if there are other terms that he/she would add to this list.

CHAPTER THREE - Essay Structure

In order for us to work on each part of the essay in detail, you need to fully understand the whole picture of the essay. Below is a very simple outline of the structure of an essay. Look at it and make sure that you understand it and if you have any questions, ask your peers and your professors. What is the difference between an essay and paragraph - GO TO THE APPENDIX TO FIND OUT!

INTRODUCTION

THESIS STATEMENT

BODY PARAGRAPH ONE
Topic Sentence

BODY PARAGRAPH TWO
Topic Sentence

BODY PARAGRAPH THREE
Topic Sentence

CONCLUSION
Restate Thesis Statement

CHAPTER FOUR - INTRODUCTIONS

At almost five thousand years old, the Djoser Step pyramid is the oldest in the world. Some say the Cuicuilco pyramids in the New World are even older than six thousand years old. What could this possibly have to do with writing in the 21st century?

Ask your mummy!
Did you laugh? This was actually considered a fairly good academic joke by the way. Thus, when you groan, just realize that professors are not very good judges of humor. We do, however, have a pretty good grasp on essay writing. Now, back to pyramids.

The shape of a pyramid provides structure that holds the massive load of the stones that reach up to forty stories into the sky (Giza was the tallest man-made building for almost 4000 years – now that is truly classical structure). This structure can be applied to logic and, therefore, to writing.

The image/shape of the pyramid is frequently used to show students the structure of the introduction and the conclusion of an essay.

INTRODUCTION PYRAMID
The introduction is like a pyramid turned upside down. Look at the diagram below. You will see an upside down pyramid.

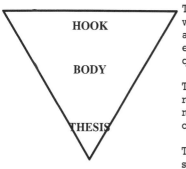

HOOK

BODY

THESIS

The wide base represents the larger idea in your writing, the greater topic. This is often referred to as the hook as it should pull people in to your essay. This is often expressed by a statistic, quotation or anecdote.

The middle of the upside down pyramid represents the body of the introduction. In the middle, you have interesting information that connects the opening to the thesis statement.

The point of the pyramid represents the thesis statement. This is the sentence at the end of the introduction which focuses your essay and tells the reader exactly what the essay will be about.

The Opening (The Hook)
As noted above, three effective ways to begin an introduction are with the use of statistics, a quotation, or an anecdote.

Hook Type One - Statistics
Read the following statistic:

A 2007 Harris poll reported that 23 percent of children felt like they were addicted to video games.

Think about what this statistic tells you. Think about what this statistic is connected do. Remember, this statistic is opening the paper, so it is a way in to the essay; it is a hook to gain the reader's attention. What might the given topic for this essay be? Is it opening an essay about children? It is opening an essay about addiction? Do the activity below to put your ideas forth.

ACTIVITY
With a partner, think about what kind of paper this statistic could open? Write down three possible **topics**.

1.

2.

3.

REFLECT
Look at the topics you and your peers came up with. Are the topics close to the statistic in content? For example, if one of your topics is video game addiction, that is fairly consistent with the content of the statistic. On the other hand, if one of your topics is childhood obesity, it is not as explicitly connected to the content of the opening statistic, but the connection is not difficult to make. In fact, it is your job in this introductory paragraph to make a connection between the opening and the topic of the essay. Thus, you can have an opening statistic that does not explicitly address the assigned topic as long as you make it relevant in your introduction.

HOOK TYPE TWO - Quotation
There is no quicker way to prove scholarship than by picking a quote from a person who has built-in respectability. In this way, you can open your paper with an idea that has been around for years and/or was said by a respected authority. Also, by attaching your ideas to a person like this, the professor unconsciously associates your great judgment with their great words!

"Am I not destroying my enemies when I make friends of them?" (Abraham Lincoln)

We've learned how to pair a statistic with a paper, and the quote is very much the same. This quote above by Lincoln might begin a paper on enemies, peace, friendship, politics or even war. Last time, you had to come up with topics for a statistic, so this time, you must find quotations that can fit a topic.

For the sake of argument, we will say the assigned topic for this paper is:

Enemies of America who later became friends of America

Find three more quotes that could open this paper.

1.
2.
3.

RESEARCH-RELATED NOTE – FINDING QUOTATIONS
It is common for students to ask where to find a quotation, so this textbook shall ask you first: where can you find quotations for your essay? Remember, you are not looking for quotations from your mother (no matter how wise she may be) or your neighbor (unless you live next door to the president). Again, the question: where can you find quotations for your essay?

Common Quotation Sources
Below are four common sources of quotations (with some overlap). Can you think of other sources?

1. Your previous learning and research
2. Your current learning and research
3. Books, newspapers - print
4. Books, newspapers, journals – online
5. Internet

In using the Internet to find quotations, it is common for students to do the following:

A. Students receive topic of essay. Topic is education.
B. Students are told to begin topic with a quotation.
C. Students go to Internet search engine like Google, Yahoo
D. Students type in the following search terms: Education quotations
E. Students gets the following results:
F. Students go to quotations.com and find a wonderful education quote by Barack Obama
G. Students take quote and put it in their essay
H. Some students remember to put quotations.com in their Works Cited page at the end of the essay

Can you see any problems (flaws, weaknesses) in this process? Now look at the revised process below.

A. Students receive topic of essay. Topic is education.
B. Students are told to begin topic with a quotation.
C. Students go to Internet search engine like Google, Yahoo
D. Students type in the following search terms: Education quotations
E. Students gets the following results:
F. Students go to quotations.com and find a wonderful education quote by Barack Obama.
G. Students ask themselves: Is that quotation correct? Did Obama really say that?
H. Students take quotation and put the whole quotation into a Search Engine with the goal of finding the original source of the quotation.
I. Students look at the search results and ignore all the hits for other quotation pages (brainyquotes.com) as students know that the these sites all copy quotations from each other. Students find a source that contains the original Obama quote.
J. Students go to the original source and examine the accuracy of the quotation and the context of the quotation. Students do not want to misquote or misrepresent the source.
K. If students are satisfied that the quotation is accurate in both words and context and that the quotation is from a reliable source, students decide to put it in their essay.
L. If students find that the quotation has errors, the meaning is not what they thought, the author is incorrect or some other information that compromises (calls into question) the quotation, students must begin the process of finding a quotation again.
M. This time, students can put a real source in their Works Cited page at the end of the essay!

HOOK TYPE THREE - Anecdote
This is a personal story that examines the writer's first-hand experience with the topic. This is the one place where first person is allowed in an academic essay. I know I just told you not to use I or we, but for the opening of an essay by anecdote, it is considered good form.

You're wondering if you can trust rules now. The short answer is no. The longer answer would bore you, but you should know that the rules are presented for your protection. If you break a rule and you're a seasoned veteran, you often get away with it. Look at the calls that Michael Jordan and Tom Brady get in their respective sports. Once you get to that level you can bend the rules. Until then, you're a rookie and you need to work very hard to raise your game within the framework of commonly accepted academic writing guidelines.

> *I awoke to the sound of thunder, a thunder that would not quit. Seconds stretched into over a minute and the earth shook maybe from the same terror that so many of us were experiencing during the Kobe earthquake of 1996.*

Notice that this might be a good opening for a paper on the power of nature or on a man's fear of the world that surrounds him or even on living in another culture.

It is important to note that an effective anecdote is relatively **short** and has a solid connection to your topic. Keeping it short is often the most difficult aspect for writers because once into your anecdote, the story takes over. You need to remember that the anecdote is not the essay; it is a way in to the essay.

PRACTICE
Using one of the topics from the previous exercises on using statistics and quotations to open an essay, write a short anecdote that could open a paper on that topic.

_____

_____

_____

_____

RECAP
You have looked at opening an essay in an interesting way and this book has suggested three possible methods - statistic, quotation, and anecdote. You have had a little practice with each, so based on that practice and on your previous writing experiences, which method do you prefer? Explain your answer.

TRANSITIONS
Even upside down, there is something between the base of the pyramid and the top of the pyramid. In fact there is more than something; there is a middle. However, before you even get to the middle, you have to get away from the opening that you spent so long figuring out. In other words, you need to transition from your interesting beginning into the topic. You can't just leave your quote, statistic or anecdote hanging there without connecting it. That would be like making vegetable soup and refusing to mix the vegetables into the broth. You can serve both separately, but everyone will say, "that's not soup." They would be right. It is two separate dishes.

The question, therefore, is how does an academic writer transition out of the opening quotation/statistic/anecdote?

Read the following two openings and note where the transitions are:

"Am I not destroying my enemies when I make friends of them?" (Abraham Lincoln.) These wise words from a great leader are still applicable today. America has experience making friends out of former enemies. In fact, the best friends of the US can be traced back to their former enemies.

A 2007 Harris poll reported that 23 percent of children felt like they were addicted to video games. Take a moment and consider that figure. If you replaced video games with alcohol or drugs in that Harris Poll result, there might very well be an uprising. With almost a quarter of children involved, video games are clearly a silent danger to society.

Notice how the transition should be two or three sentences maximum and that you've set the course for your thesis with this move away from the broadest part of the paper.

Here are ten inspirational quotes. Choose three and practice transitioning into a paper about education. Remember, you are not at the thesis, and you are not even in the body.

ACTIVITY

1. Mark Twain
Twenty years from now you will be more disappointed by the things that you didn't do than by the ones you did do. So throw off the bowlines. Sail away from the safe harbor. Catch the trade winds in your sails. Explore. Dream. Discover.

2. Luigi Pirandello
In bed my real love has always been the sleep that rescued me by allowing me to dream.

3. Dr. Martin Luther King Jr.
Take the first step in faith. You don't have to see the whole staircase, just take the first step.

4. Zig Ziglar
People often say that motivation doesn't last. Well, neither does bathing - that's why we recommend it daily.

5. T. S. Elliot
Only those who will risk going too far can possibly find out how far one can go.

6. Buddha
All that we are is the result of what we have thought.

7. Ralph Waldo Emerson
Do not go where the path may lead, go instead where there is no path and leave a trail.

8. Peter F. Drucker
We know nothing about motivation. All we can do is write books about it.

9. Nora Roberts
If you don't go after what you want, you'll never have it. If you don't ask, the answer is always no. If you don't step forward, you're always in the same place.

10. Stephen Covey
Begin with the end in mind.

The Body of the Introduction

You are now ready to enter the middle, or the body, of your introduction. Many students think that the transition from the opening hook is the middle and the thesis can follow directly. However, that is not the case. You need something more in the middle; while the introduction is not the whole paper, you still need to work toward your thesis rather than sprint.

In the middle part of your pyramid, you have to prove that your paper will be interesting. Interesting makes the reader want to continue and as you are very near the beginning of your essay, it is important to be interesting. Too many students just tread water in the middle of their introductions and never take the time to explain the significance of the paper, of their writing, to the reader. In your mind, video games might be about to take over the consciousness of an entire generation and the content could be damaging. Perhaps, you have seen that war might be the cycle by which international relationships are forged. Possibly, you can predict that earthquakes are coming to your city! Admittedly, the last one might be a bit sensational, but you should be able to see that the body of your introduction needs to connect the reader to your topic. It is this connection that makes the reader care. Then, both you and the reader will be ready for the point of your pyramid, the thesis. You will look more closely at the middle after a quick review below of the thesis statement.

Thesis Statement

For now the position of the thesis is set in stone (yes that's a pyramid jest). It is the last sentence of the introduction. Notice that the thesis should be a single sentence. If for example your thesis is two sentences make it one. Notice also that it comes at the end of the introduction. If your thesis is somewhere else in the introduction, put it at the end.

As you establish trust with your instructor, they may alter these rules or abolish them altogether, but until you have a strong writing background, stick to the architecture that has been around for thousands of years. It is indeed solid.

SAMPLES FROM THE REAL WORLD

The first example is from an assignment asking students to find three reasons for the greatness of a leader. The second example is from an assignment asking students to analyze the changes in Phil Connors the protagonist in the movie Groundhog Day.

As you read, mark the following on the text (underline, highlight, use margin notes):

- ❖ The opening hook of the introduction
- ❖ The transition away from the opening to the body
- ❖ The body of the introduction
- ❖ The transition from the body to the thesis
- ❖ The thesis

REAL WORLD EXAMPLE ONE

It is estimated by New Harbinger Publications that almost 15 percent of all adults in the United States, or almost thirty-one million people, struggle with personality disorders that alter actions and behaviors. Similarly, the main characters in Nathaniel Hawthorne's *The Birthmark* and Edgar Allan Poe's *The Cask of Amontillado* suffer from personality disorders that influence their obsessive behavior and relationship with others. In *The Birthmark* scientist Aylmer temporarily leaves his laboratory to marry the beautiful Georgiana but grows fixated on the birthmark found on Georgiana's cheek and the apparent removal of it from her near perfect face, regardless of cost. Poe's work similarly deals with fixation by introducing Montresor, the main character, who is fixated on murdering a fellow Italian nobleman Fortunado for insulting him previously. In doing so,

Montresor essentially shows no remorse toward his victim. The short stories written by both Hawthorne and Poe mirror ideals through the use of similar somber stories or plots based on fixation, mentally unstable obsessive characters, and similar dark and dismal settings as the background for the action in each of the plots.

ANALYZE

1. Find the hook. Identify its type.
2. Find the transition.
3. Find the body of the introduction
4. Find the thesis statement.
5. What are the strengths of this introduction?
6. What are the weaknesses of this introduction?

REAL WORLD EXAMPLE TWO

"Character isn't something you were born with and can't change, like your fingerprints. It's something you weren't born with and must take responsibility for forming."(Rohn). Jim Rohn, who is an American business philosopher, motivational counselor, and businessman, believes that character is not a genetic feature that you born with. Character can be changed if a person intends to do so and works on it. By the same token James A. Froude said "You cannot dream yourself into a character; you must hammer and forge yourself one". The meaning of these two quotations was clearly illustrated in the movie Groundhog Day. In the movie, actor Bill Murray played Phil, an arrogant, selfish weather forecaster who traveled to Punxsutawney, Pennsylvania, to do a broadcast on the Groundhog Day festivities. During the movie, Phil discovered that he was trapped in a time loop where he experienced the same day's events over and over. At the beginning, Murray's character (Phil) responded with confusion and despair. As days pass, Phil's despair deepens and he begins to spend his days trying to kill himself. After many failed attempts at killing himself, Phil realized that he can not change the circumstances. Knowing that he can not change the surrounding circumstances, Phil

worked on himself and changed his personality. By the end of the Groundhog Day movie,

Phil was able to change himself from a selfish, sarcastic, and negative person to a

selfless, respectful, and optimistic person.

ANALYZE

1. Find the hook. Identify its type.
2. Find the transition.
3. Find the body of the introduction
4. Find the thesis statement.
5. What are the strengths of this introduction?
6. What are the weaknesses of this introduction?

IN-CLASS ACTIVITY

STEP ONE - COMPARE IN PAIRS

Get into pairs and compare your analysis of the two paragraphs. Look at the opening, the body and the thesis of each introduction and see if you can identify where each paragraph has strengths and weaknesses (both have strengths and weaknesses but one is certainly preferable over the other).

STEP ONE - COMPARE IN GROUPS

Group with another pair and discuss your methods for taking apart the two introductions. Review the main elements and see if either group has found something unique. See if your group can find a flaw or correction that none of the other groups can. What part of the weakest introduction is in the most need of a rewrite? What part of the stronger introduction is particularly thoughtful?

If you have extra time, find a better quote for each paper.

WEB OR EMAIL SPECIAL

Choose one of the two thesis statements below and write an introduction of at least 300 words with a quote, stat or anecdote as the first sentence. Remember to apply what you learned in this chapter about transitions, the body, and the thesis (the last sentence of your paragraph). Follow your instructor's directions for the finished introduction (bring to class, post on class website, email).

1. The primary parking problems at this college are cost, availability, and location.
2. The governor has made several errors in policy but the most damaging are in tax policy, job policy and education policy.

EXTRA CREDIT OPPORTUNITY
Copy and paste the content of this introduction that you wrote into a template for a business letter and then send it to the local paper as a letter to the editor. Extra credit if someone in class gets their letter published.

CHAPTER FIVE
THESIS STATEMENTS

In the previous chapter, you learned the basic of the thesis statement, but in this chapter, you are going to gain a little more insight into the thesis.

The original use of thesis came to us handed down from the terminology of music. It meant the accented or most important stress in a string of words. The modern thesis statement is less American Idol and more CNN commentary. It seeks to give the reader a specific idea of the opinion of the writer on an important topic. Most students would stop me right there and say they have never had an important topic given to them in a writing class! This is a common problem or false assumption, so let's get it out of the way right now. Look at the following topic:

Modern Art

This is probably the hardest topic to sell to a student, and yet I want to show you why you should be buying it. A complete education for a student is no more of a matter of choice than a balanced diet is for a teenager. If I had had my choice of what I could eat for every meal when I was young, I would have gladly lived in a van outside of the local Cinnabon. Would that be a mature idea? No. Would that help me later in life? No. The secret is to find something about the topic that you can invest in. So, let's get back to Modern Art.

What about a paper showing the three most expensive pieces of modern art sold this year? Wouldn't you like to see them?

How about an essay that seeks to show that at least three of the modern artists of this generation are frauds? That might be interesting.

The most important thing to realize is that there is no such thing as a bad topic. There are imaginative and interesting ways to look at almost any problem that a young (or old) mind comes into contact with. That is the spark. You come up against a new problem and you look at it in your own way. It is much too easy to give in to familiarity especially while you are doing exercises and learning the structure. However, strive not to submit to the obvious even while you learn the structure of how to write your thesis statements. More importantly, your thesis statement will reflect the effort you made to approach the topic in an interesting and less obvious way.

Now, after that mini lecture on how there are no boring topics, let's return to thesis statements.

IN-CLASS EXERCISE
Thesis Statement Analysis

As you know, a thesis statement is the sentence in your essay that communicates the main idea of your paper. The thesis statement is central to the reader understanding the purpose and focus of your essay. It is, in short, extremely important. A good thesis statement possesses certain characteristics that make it effective as the central, controlling idea governing all of the information in the body of the essay. There are certain things a thesis can and cannot be.

A thesis statement should not be:

- ❑ A fact
- ❑ A question
- ❑ An announcement
- ❑ Too broad (is it too big for an essay)
- ❑ Too narrow (can it be developed)
- ❑ A fragment

Read the following thesis statements and decide if they are good or if they are inadequate. Be prepared to explain your choice. Use the qualities described above to indicate why the statement is weak.

1. In the past ten years, the crime rate in the United States has decreased, but the prison population has increased.

2. Love is important.

3. Now I am going to discuss why Obama should be re-elected.

4. Harsh punishments for teenagers will discourage them from turning to a life of crime.

5. Pepsi is used as a pesticide in some parts of the world.

6. In 2000, American taxpayers spent approximately $23,000 a year to keep an inmate in prison.

7. Let's discuss why the Internet is a necessary evil.

8. Music is a reflection of people's souls.

Now you will practice writing thesis statements.

We will go over the example together. You don't need to fill in each part; some people work best in a process sequence; others can go straight from a broad subject to a specific thesis. Do what works for you. If you aren't sure, try both ways. The one rule is that the thesis statements must be EXPLICIT. That means you must list the three main points of your essay in your thesis.

Subject: An addictive habit
Narrowed subject: smoking marijuana
Controlling idea: smoking marijuana – relaxed me, provided escape, alienated family

Thesis Statement: While smoking marijuana has clear short-term benefits of relaxation and escapism, the alienation of friends and family can be too high a price to pay.

STEP ONE - WRITE
Write explicit thesis statements for each of the topics below.

Subject: An addictive habit

Narrowed subject:

Controlling idea:

Thesis Statement:

Subject: Internet Research

Narrowed subject:

Controlling idea:

Thesis Statement:

Subject: Modern Art

Narrowed subject:

Controlling idea:

Thesis Statement:

Subject: Community colleges

Narrowed subject:

Controlling idea:

Thesis Statement:

Subject: Voting

Narrowed subject:

Controlling idea:

Thesis Statement:

Subject: Video Games

Narrowed subject:

Controlling idea:

Thesis Statement:

Subject: Technology in education

Narrowed subject:

Controlling idea:

Thesis Statement:

STEP TWO - SHARE

Find a partner, exchange books (papers, emails) and review each of your partner's thesis statements. For each one, answer the following:

1. Is the thesis statement explicit?
2. Is the thesis statement one complete sentence?
3. Is the thesis statement on topic?
4. Is the thesis written in clear accurate grammar?
5. Does the writer use the first person singular?

If you are still unsure about the thesis statement, ask your instructor for further practice.

THESIS STATEMENT versus TOPIC SENTENCE

Some students confuse thesis statements and topic sentences, so let's clarify the two and make sure that you are clear about the difference.

A thesis statement is the sentence that identifies the main idea of an essay; thesis statements spend their time organizing essays of more than one paragraph. A topic sentence is the sentence that identifies the main idea of a paragraph; topic sentences keep the individual paragraphs on track. Yes, it is that simple. Now, let's repeat that information again.

A thesis statement contains the main idea that you will be presenting in your essay. Many colleges promote the five-paragraph essay form and have students advance themselves in that form of writing. When writing a five-paragraph essay, the thesis statement belongs at the end of the introduction. It can be explicit or implicit. An explicit thesis statement contains the sub-points of the essay. An implicit thesis statement does not contain any sub-points. On the other hand, a topic sentence is the first sentence of a paragraph and it contains the main idea of that paragraph. If the thesis statement listed the sub-points, then the topic sentence in each paragraph of that essay will contain one of those sub-points. All of this information can be seen in the following table.

	THESIS STATEMENT	TOPIC SENTENCE
PURPOSE	A thesis statement is the sentence that presents the main idea for the whole essay.	A topic sentence presents the main idea of a paragraph.
FORM 1 **Explicit**	Can be explicit and contain sub-points Example: Lindsay Lohan's current predicament is a result of poor parenting skills, inappropriate friend choice, and strong self-loathing.	Contains the sub-point given in the thesis Example: The first reason why Lindsay Lohan is currently in prison is her parents and their blatant inability and unwillingness to discipline her.
FORM 2 **Implicit**	Can be implicit and not state the sub-points. Example: Lindsay Lohan's current predicament can be traced to three key factors in her life and personality.	Contains the sub-point NOT stated in the thesis Example: The first reason why Lindsay Lohan is currently in prison is her parents and their blatant inability and unwillingness to discipline her.
LOCATION	End of the Introduction	Beginning of the paragraph

SPECIFIC EXAMPLES

From the example below, you can see that writing a good explicit thesis statement also means you have all three of your topic sentences written as well. Look at the sub-points from the thesis and you can see that they are also present in the topic sentences for each body paragraph.

EXAMPLE ONE

Thesis
Rome fell because of pressure from the barbarians, a stagnant economy and a lack of political leadership.

Topic Sentence 1 (For Body Paragraph One)
One Reason Rome Fell Was The Pressure From The Northern Tribes Of The Verangeans.

Topic Sentence 2 (For Body Paragraph Two)
Another cause of Rome's demise was the economy.

Topic Sentence 3 (For Body Paragraph Three)
Perhaps the largest problem that led to Rome's downfall was the political leadership or lack thereof at the time.

EXAMPLE TWO

Thesis
Electric cars have not been successful because they have little power, they are dangerous to drive, and lastly they are very expensive.

Topic Sentence 1
Electric cars have not been a success in the market because of their lack of power.

Topic Sentence 2
Secondly, most electric cars are extremely small and potentially lethal.

Topic Sentence 3
Lastly, electric cars are incredibly expensive.

In-class Activity

Write an explicit thesis statement and three topic sentences for each of the following subjects:

1. Problems with your school
2. How to save money on the Internet
3. Great scientists
4. Great bands of the 2000's (or choose a decade)

The first one has been started for you.
Examples of problems with your school

Thesis Statement:

_____, _____ and _____ are three major problems with _____.

Topic sentence 1

A large problem with this school is that it _____

Topic sentence 2

Another problem with this institution is a complete lack of _____.

Topic sentence 3

Perhaps the biggest problem with _____ is _____.

Now you finish the remaining three. Once you are done, share them with your peers and instructor for feedback.

WRITING BREAK 2
Tone

It is a little too easy in a writing course to leave some of the writing tips to the Appendix. That doesn't always help you as a writer, so throughout the text there will be writing breaks just like this one. This writing break focuses on Tone and Voice.

Tone and Rules
Look back at the examples of formal writing (not journals) given thus far in the text and you will notice that not one of them includes the use of the first or the second person. In other words, not one of them uses any of the following:

"I" "You" "We" "Us" "Our" "My"

This bothers some students as they don't understand why they cannot write "*I think that the president should have more power*" when they want to express their ideas. Consider the following two statements:

> *I think that the president should have more power.*

> *The president should have more power.*

Is there any difference in meaning? No.

Is there any difference in tone? Yes.

The first is personal and that means it could be said anywhere – at a party, on the phone, in a blog, in a text. It could be followed by an explanation or it could be followed by an invitation to a movie about monkeys.
The second one is not personal; it is an opinion that is expressed for a reader who is going to expect more information. In other words, it is a more academic expression of an opinion. You are in college. College is part of the academic world and as a college student, you need to show that you understand and can master the conventions of that academic world. Now, of course if the assignment is a narrative or a description and demands a personal and informal tone, then you show your mastery of academic conventions by adhering to the assignment. However, if the assignment is an academic essay, an informal and academic voice is best.

PERSONAL EXERCISE
Do a search of any of your essays for these terms. Did you find any? If you did, does that mean you made a mistake or was it part of the assignment?

FROM INFORMAL...

My three favorite flavors of ice cream are: vanilla, chocolate and crispy choco-nilla chunk.

TO FORMAL...

The best flavors available at Baskin Robins are vanilla, chocolate and crispy choco-nilla chunk.

INFORMAL

FORMAL

In the informal presentation, the readers are left with the feeling that the writer is not being objective. It's just his taste. Since they are different than he is, it might not be valuable information.

In the formal presentation, the readers don't need to know the writer to see the importance. They just have to be customers of Baskin Robins who value input.

Do you see how the subtle difference might be what separates a person reading and learning from you and a person choosing to ignore your carefully presented opinion? I want your words to be packed with so much thought and insight that they change the reader into a crispy choco-nilla junkie. Using a more formal presentation scheme increases the odds of that.

INTERNET ACTIVITY
STEP ONE
Find an article of at least 500 words. Complete the following information for that article:
Source of Article:
Title of Article:
Author:
Date published:
Full reference for Article (so anyone can find it):

STEP TWO

Print the article, so you have a copy to show your peers and instructor.

STEP THREE

In one to four sentences   answer the following:
Analyze the tone of the article   you read. How would you describe the tone?
Give support from the reading.

_____

_____

_____

_____

_____

Like everything, practice is the key and the more you analyze tone, the more alert you are to changes in different articles and writings. That gives you an insight into writing and writers that you will ultimately be able to use, too.

TONE CHANGE PRACTICE

Remember the paragraph you wrote in Chapter One (page 18) in which you had to write about your life. You brought the paragraph to class or posted in on the website. Take that paragraph and convert it from first person singular to third person singular. In other words, take it from personal to impersonal. Instead of "I", use your name and she or he. Get the idea? If you are not sure, ask a peer or the instructor for help.

Chapter 6 CONCLUSIONS

Now it's time to turn the pyramid back to its traditional posture. It is easier to think about building this one and actually it is usually easier to write a conclusion. The ABCs of writing a conclusion are in the diagram above.

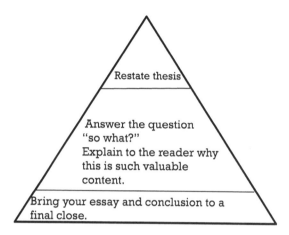

The first sentence   usually restates the thesis. Notice that it does not say, repeat the thesis word for word; restate it. Put it into different words from your thesis but maintain the meaning. Make sure you list the three subtopics that you covered in the paper. It is strangely reassuring that the writer remembers what he just wrote about. Comfort your reader.

Next, go on to explain why the paper is so important. Remember, you do this in the third person and not in the first person. One of the key things to remember is that this is not just an exercise in putting forth your own point of view. It is a litmus test for whether or not your paper is really important to the reader.

If you have difficulties writing this part of the conclusion it is probably due to a weak or obvious essay. For example, let's say you wrote about how bad smoking is for health. Well, you get to this section and realize that you have really chosen a topic that everyone already knows about. Your ideas might have furthered the conversation, and if they did, you are still fine. However, if you didn't break any new ground in your research, it is time to switch your topic. Hey, it only took writing the entire paper to find out! Let's face it though, it is better to find that out before your grade comes back.

ENDING STYLE 1 – FUTURE PREDICTION

Finally, the ending comment is really a matter of style. Some people like to go out with a future prediction.

If people do not stop dumping pharmaceuticals into public water sources, the ecosystem will be changed and change is not always good for the top of the food chain. Ask the dinosaurs.

ENDING STYLE 2 – CALL TO ACTION

Others like to end with a call to action.

Stop buying individually packaged foods. The plastic that wraps the daily lunch food of children will be around when their grandchildren retire.

Whatever you choose, make sure it forms a wide base. Make a comment that broadens your argument to include every reader. A conclusion really tests to see if the writer has a point of view, express it here with conviction and your paper will have a strong foundation.

IN-CLASS ACTIVITY

Use the topics below to practice both kinds of conclusion endings - call to action and future predictions. Write both types of concluding comments for each paper topic.

1. A paper about the dangers of handguns.

2. A paper about the positive aspects of a current politician.

3. A paper about the worst food in your city. (Please don't predict medical consequences unless you are pre-med).

WRITING BREAK 3

Some Important Rules

The Rule of Three

I often get the question of why essays need to have three body paragraphs, three main supporting points, and a three-part thesis statement. Once I get past my initial urge to say "because they do" (English professors have the same youthful impulses of retort) I actually started examining the problem. I think the story below illustrates my point better than a lecture.

I walked into class one day and found a young woman wearing UGG boots. She was showing them off to others in the class. I asked the class if they liked them and they said yes. I then asked them if the lady wearing them was proof that UGG boots were popular on campus. Some said yes, some said no. I had to agree with those who said no. If there's only one person in a classroom with the boots, it was probably just the fashion choice of one student. Does that make it popular? If I looked around the room I could see several individual fashion choices (including one with a young man's boxer shorts which I will never understand) and unless I would count all of them as being popular, I couldn't count the UGG boots as popular. The next day, two girls were wearing UGG boots. I brought it up to the class and more people agreed that it meant that they were popular. I was still unconvinced. I noticed that two boys wore baseball caps and everyone agreed that baseball caps were not prevalent on campus. I was stuck. I agreed that there was a trend, but not very solid proof of popularity.

Later in the semester, someone in class noticed that three girls were wearing the same boots. Now, in such a small sample of people to have three wearing the same brand of shoes made a pretty good case for popularity. The rule of three convinces people. Think about it. If two of your professors drove Mini Coopers you'd think they MIGHT be professor mobiles. But if three of your professors owned the Cooper, you'd be convinced that for some reason Profs loved the Mini.

The point, therefore, is that three is the minimum number of points you should be using to support your thesis. Two just isn't enough, as noted above, to make it more than a trend.

Paragraph Rules

Don't write a paragraph of fewer than seven sentences. You want to seem like you are being complete. The academic paragraph must comprise at least half of a page. If it looks like you have too little to say in a paragraph, the reader gets concerned about your balance. Did you really write a thesis with three parts or did you write one with two parts and a short addendum? Do not worry about your paragraph looking two long; I can guarantee you that it won't be considered too long if everything you write remains on topic.

Internet Rules
Use the Internet, but don't quote the Internet. If you can't find an author – it shouldn't be used as a source in your work. This includes Encyclopedia, quote websites and the ever popular advocacy sites. If there is not a published expert that contributes to the website, it is not a good source of support. Go to the library, or search complete texts at Google books. Don't get caught in the idea that the Internet is a shortcut to research. It often gets a student off track and presents ideas with little basis.

EMAIL OR WEB SPECIAL

Place the following in your Facebook update box or send it via email to all of the friends you have in school.

I'm doing a survey of the rules of different classrooms. Please post or respond with some of the rules that you've experienced in class. Be specific if you can.

Collect all of the responses and see if a pattern develops when you meet with your classmates next time. Spend the first ten minutes looking over the rules that people have found. Are there differences between disciplines? Are there differences between generations? Why do you think that instructors make rules and why do you think that students often fail to follow them?

The Writing Modules

The second half of this book is broken down into Writing Modules. Each module takes students through the process of writing an essay in a specific rhetorical mode:

Exposition Essay
Classification Essay
Cause or Effect Essay
Comparison or Contrast Essay
Argument Essay

In each of these modules, students do exercises, Internet/Email specials, writing practices, and learn a little more specifically about each mode and how with a little tweaking all that they learned in the first half is relevant and applicable to every essay they write.

There is no specific order in which these modules ought to be done. That is and should be driven by the instructor. Each module stands alone. Some modules have a theme; some do not. All work to make students better understand essay writing and all provide practice. After all, writing is practice.

Writing Module One

THE EXPOSITION ESSAY

Definition

Typically, an expository essay has the purpose of informing, explaining, describing, or defining the subject to the reader. Don't be too confused because you will often see chapters in text books on Definition Essays and Descriptive Essays. In this book, an expository or exposition essay is simply an essay in which the writer explains something. It is a good place to begin with essay writing because it eases students into the structure of the essay in an easy style.

The topic for this module is Successful Learners and Successful Learning. The activities lead to producing an essay connected to this topic.

STEP ONE - READ AND RESPOND

Read the following paragraph on becoming a successful learner and then respond to the reading.

Becoming A Successful Learner by Dr. M. Dembo

Educational research has indicated that learners' self-perceptions about learning play an important role in determining their academic success. Self-perceptions refer to the attitudes, values, and beliefs that students bring to the learning environment. For example, some students have the belief that procrastination is a personality trait that can't be changed. Other students believe that changes in personal behavior can reduce procrastination and lead to the attainment of certain goals. Think about how these two different beliefs can lead to different learning outcomes. Many of the beliefs you bring to community college were formed during your K-12 learning experiences even if those experiences were a long time ago. Some of your beliefs will help you become a more successful learner, while other beliefs (and this may surprise you) may hinder your academic success.

Respond to the following:

Write one sentence, using your own words as much as possible, explaining what this paragraph is about.

_____

Write one or two questions that this paragraph answers.

_____

_____

_____

Read the following short paragraph

Academic success in college requires the use of certain learning and motivational strategies. Dembo and Seli (2008) point out that successful learners are not simply individuals who know more than others. In fact, successful learners possess more effective learning strategies for accessing and using their knowledge, motivate themselves, and make changes in their behavior when they have difficulty learning. Educators describe these students as self-regulated. Learners with self-regulation skills find a way to learn and remove obstacles that interfere with their learning. Before you learn how to self-regulate your behavior, you must first be able to self-observe and self-evaluate your present academic behavior. This task is important because you bring many skills that will help you succeed. In addition, you may determine that you need to acquire some new learning strategies to help you succeed, not only in this class, but also in college.

Respond to the following:
Write one sentence, using your own words as much as possible, explaining what this paragraph is about.

_____

Write one or two questions that this paragraph answers.

_____

_____

_____

STEP TWO - DISCUSS AND DEBATE
Analyze Your Beliefs About Learning and Motivation (Adapted from Dembo and Seli, 2008). There are many ways to do this discussion activity. Here are two options.

Option One - Mobile Debate

7. The instructor will divide the class into the YES side and the NO side.
8. Students must then stand up.
9. The instructor will read one of the following statements below and you must move to either the YES side of the classroom or the NO side of the classroom. You may not stand in the middle. You may not be undecided.
10. The instructor can move from statement to statement quickly and make notes or the instructor can stop after a statement and ask you to explain your belief. Students may change sides after hearing other students' opinions.

Option Two - Read and Discuss

1. Read each of the following statements.
2. Place the corresponding letter or letters whether you agree (A), disagree (D).
3. Discuss your ratings with other students in your class.
4. After identifying your beliefs, think about how they influence your motivation and learning.

__1. "I can't do well in a course if I'm not interested in the content."

__2. "I will not learn much if I am bored in class."

__3. "Competition is a great motivator."

__4. "Human intelligence is fixed early in life."

__5. "If I simply listen in class and read my assignments I should do well in college."

__6. "The most important aspect of studying is finding enough time."

__7. "The key to success in college is having good instructors."

---8. 'If I have to work hard on a task, it usually means that I am not very smart."

__9. "If I email the instructor a question about an assignment and he/she does not

respond, I don't need to finish the assignment."

__ 10. "Getting nervous about tests and exams often leads to my failure in a course."

STEP THREE - READ MORE, REFLECT, PERSONALIZE

Read the following

When we start to look at our behavior and move to change it, it is easy to believe that simply by taking a few steps and telling ourselves that we are doing it, it will indeed be done. However, in truth, without reflection upon what we are doing or what we have done, we miss a key component of the process. In fact, by taking the time to reflect upon our actions, we can work to make the change real.

Let's look at an example. Your house or living space is always messy. You decide you will keep it tidy, but you know that you have to start small and you decide to keep the coffee table in the center of the room clean and free from clutter. This is easy for the first few days when your motivation is high and you are clearly tied to your goal. Then, you get busier, life sets back in, and two weeks later, the coffee table is back to its original state. Now, you may have valid reasons for letting it get messy again, but consider this: if you had tried to monitor and **reflect** on what you were doing and were not doing and why, you would have had the opportunity to see what was happening and what was preventing you from clearing the coffee table. Take a moment and think of another example which seems to fit this scenario – it can be academic, social, personal – and if you want to, share it with the group.

EXERCISE
Choose one of the beliefs related to learning that you discussed in class and explain how it influences your behavior. Be specific. Choose another belief (of your own, not discussed in class) and analyze how it influences your behavior. Be specific.

WRITING ASSIGNMENT
Due Date: _____

Write a paragraph of at least 400 words explaining one of the beliefs discussed in class and its potential impacts on a student's learning. Although you may draw on your personal experiences and perceptions, this is not a personal paragraph, so use third person singular (or plural) and maintain an academic tone. The paragraph must contain all of the following elements.

- Clear topic sentence
- At least three main supporting points
- Specific details to support the main points.
- A concluding sentence

Your paragraph must be typed and double spaced.

STEP FOUR - DISCOVERING MORE ON SELF-REGULATED LEARNING

Select a student in your class. Your assignment is to interview each other regarding the six components of self-regulation. They are listed below.

Components of Self-Regulation

1. *Motivation* –The ability to self-motivate your thoughts and behavior when necessary.
2. *Use of Time*-The ability to plan how to use your time so that your goals are attained.
3. *Methods of Learning* – The ability to use different learning strategies for different academic tasks.
4. *Control of one's physical environment.* The ability to modify or change one's study environment to improve concentration and to complete academic tasks.
5. *Control of one's social environment.* The ability to seek help from peers, instructors, tutoring centers, and/or textbooks or reference materials when needed.
6. *Monitoring performance* – The ability to evaluate one's work to determine progress toward meeting personal, social, occupational, or learning goals.

INTERVIEW PROCESS
An interview with no focus or forethought is will not serve you well here, so follow the list of steps in order to conduct an effective and satisfying interview.

1. Choose a partner to interview. If not interviewing in class time, set up a time and place for you to meet and complete the interview. Your instructor may have recommendations for you on this.
2. Devise a series of questions to ask your peer. The question must help you obtain information about your colleague's self-regulation skills. Remember, there are six components. After asking him/her your questions, ask your partner to determine which areas of self-regulation he/she considers to be strengths and which areas he/she considers to be weaknesses or areas for improvement.
3. Review questions. Find another student and review the questions with him/her. Do not use the person you will interview. If you have any questions, talk to your instructor.
4. When your questions are ready, show the instructor and get his/her permission to proceed.
5. Review interview time and place with your partner. Exchange phone numbers.
6. Meet and interview.
7. After interviewing your colleague, let your colleague interview you. He/she will have different questions but a similar goal.
8. Bring your interview results to class. Your instructor will guide you on the form of the results (a paragraph, a list, a presentation, a summary).

STEP FIVE - IN-CLASS DISCUSSION ON INTERVIEWS

In your interview pairs, discuss the results of your interviews. Take it in turns to address the following:

What did you learn about your partner in terms of self-regulation and the six components of self-regulation? As your partner tells you his/her interview results, listen carefully before you agree or disagree. This is not a judgment. It's a subjective interview result, so don't take things personally. After listening to your partner, explain what you agree or disagree with and work out how he/she came to those conclusions.

STEP SIX - SELF-ANALYSIS

Analyze Your Learning and Studying Behavior (Adapted from Dembo and Seli, 2008) (in small groups)
Directions: For each question, place a check in the corresponding box that best describes the strategies you presently use to complete your reading assignments and take class notes. This is not a test, so don't judge which answers you think are the "best"; be honest about what you do and how you do it.

	Always	Sometimes	Never
1. I preview all my textbooks to review the learning aids provided by the authors.			
2. I think of questions as I read.			
3. I underline my textbook as I read.			
4. I look for main ideas as I read.			
5. I make notes to identify material I don't understand.			
6. I complete exercises or answer questions at the end of each chapter when I am finished reading.			
7. I constantly monitor my understanding as I read.			
8. I condense the main ideas in a lecture rather than write complete sentences.			
9. I daydream during lectures.			
10. I separate main ideas from examples and other secondary information during lectures			
11. I try to determine the organization of the lecture.			
12. I review my notes each day after class.			
13. I make a notation in my notes for information I don't understand.			

As you look at the results of your self-analysis, can you tie any of these things to the six components of self-regulated learning? Can you make any connections both in general and for you personally?

STEP SEVEN - LOOKING AT OTHERS
CASE STUDIES FOR ANALYSIS

Read the following paragraph on self-regulated learning and then read the three case studies. At the end of each case study, there are questions for discussion.

Students can be taught to become more self-regulated learners by acquiring specific strategies that are both successful for them and that enable them to increase their control over their own behavior and environment. Most researchers agree that the best learning occurs when someone carefully observes and considers his own behaviors and acts upon what he has learned. This means that students learn to decrease negative behaviors and increase positive behaviors. Therefore, students who are self-regulated must learn to continually ask themselves "Does this strategy work for me in this situation?" In order to self-regulate, students must shift their focus from comparing their performance to peers to self-comparisons, and from being reactive to being proactive learners. Goals direct activities, and students must learn that there are different ways to attain goals, and how to select the best way to complete a specific task. In many classrooms, teachers assume most of the responsibility for the learning process and students may begin to depend on this model of learning.(National Research Center on the Gifted and Talented)

Case Study 1 (This is taken from the National Research Center on the Gifted and Talented at the University of Connecticut. Please visit their excellent training website to see this case study and more information on strategies for helping students and self-regulated behavior. At the following link, you can see the introduction and download the pdf version of their presentation and training http://www.gifted.uconn.edu/siegle/SelfRegulation/index.htm).

Maria is an eighth grade student who was identified as gifted in first grade. She read at the seventh grade level by the time she finished second grade and has always scored at the 99% on all areas on standardized achievement tests. She excels in language arts, but has extremely high scores across all areas. Maria does not like math and had coasted through the math curriculum from first through seventh grade, doing minimal homework and getting top grades. Because of her scores on achievement tests and previous grades, she is recommended for an advanced algebra class in eighth grade and encounters, for her first time in school, some challenge in mathematics. She struggles with a few concepts and begins to tell her parents that she is really not smart. She quits whenever she finds a homework problem she can not solve while doing homework and tells her parents she will ask the teacher the next day for help. She continues to do her homework each time it is assigned, but completes only the problems that she can easily do and gets help from her friends and teacher the next day if she can not quickly and correctly solve a problem. The answers to problems are in the back of the book so that after a few minutes of work, if she has not solved the problem, she looks it up in the back of the book but fails to learn how to solve the problem. She fails two tests, becomes convinced she is terrible at math and considers dropping out of the algebra class.

How can she gain the self-regulation skills she needs to succeed in a more challenging class?

CASE STUDY 2 (This case study, with a name change, is taken from a Counseling course at College of the Canyons. Authors include Alonso, E., Hooper, G., Martin, J. Maple C.)

On Sunday night Catherine reviews her work for the coming week and writes some short-term goals that she would like to accomplish. She then opens her weekly calendar and determines how much time is needed to complete her tasks. Catherine works 10 hours a week and realizes that she needs more time to prepare for her midterm in biology the following Monday. She makes plans to study for the exam on Monday, Wednesday and Sunday. She realizes that her family is planning to attend her niece's birthday party next Sunday afternoon, but she needs the time to prepare for the exam. She calls her aunt to tell her that she can't attend the party on Sunday.
On Monday, Catherine contacts two students in her biology class and asks them if they would be interested in forming a study group to review some possible questions that she thinks may be on the exam. She tells her two friends to their possible exam questions so that they all would be prepared for the study session. She also calls the library where she can reserve a study room for her group. After the study session on Monday, Catherine and her friends determine that they have many unanswered questions about the blood circulation of the human heart. They write down these questions and decide that one of them would go to the instructor's office hours to get the questions answered and then email the instructor's response to the rest of the group.After her study session on Sunday afternoon, Catherine reviews all the material that will be on the exam the next day and makes a list of content material she feels that she doesn't fully understand. She reviews the course syllabus, notes, and textbook and decides that he needs to review two chapters in her textbook and a few lecture notes Sunday evening before she is ready for the exam on Monday.

Is Catherine a self-regulated learner? Which of the six components does Catherine employ in her learning and behavior?

CASE STUDY 2 (This case study, with a name change, is taken from a Counseling course at College of the Canyons. Authors include Alonso, E., Hooper, G., Martin, J. Maple C.)

Jan is a freshman at the College of the Canyons who want to transfer to UCLA to enter their journalism program. She recently purchased a car and feels that she has many expenses that need to be paid. As a result, she agrees to work 25 hours a week at the local Fry's Electronics store. Jan sometimes works evenings so her best time for study is early in the morning and late in the afternoon. She usually attempts to complete his reading assignments early in the morning. However, she is often tired and finds it difficult to concentrate. Since she doesn't have a computer at home, she uses the computers in the library to complete his writing assignments. However, she often finds it difficult to get to the library during her free time. As a result, she attempts to complete her assignments at her boy friend's house. She spends time talking with her boy friend and often finds that the time goes by very fast and she needs to go to work before his assignment is completed.

Jan would like to complete his work by herself even though her instructor has office hours. She doesn't want her instructor to think she is not capable; therefore she rather asks friends for help than meeting with her instructor. When Jan studies for exams, she rereads his textbook and notes even though she admits that sometimes she doesn't understand some of the notes she takes. She often complains that her English instructor speaks too fast and taking notes is very difficult in her class. *Is Jan a self-regulated learner? Which of the six components does Jan employ in his learning and behavior?*

STEP EIGHT - BACK TO YOU

Now you have read about self-regulated learning behaviors and you have been interviewed and you have conducted a self-analysis, so what does it all mean? Well, that is what you get to decide. Now, you get to self-reflect (remember that little reading earlier on the importance of self-reflection in the process of changing behavior?).

PERSONAL WRITING ASSIGNMENT

In your journal, on your wiki page, on your website, in a traditional paper format, (follow your instructors directions) complete the following. Although it is personal, keep it structured. It could easily be three paragraphs. It should be about two pages typed and double spaced. It is personal, so you can use I.

Based on the interview results, your own analysis, and your own self-reflections, how much of a self-regulated learner are you? What areas of your own behavior could you improve upon? Do you think you will do that? If so, how will you make the necessary changes? If not, why not?

DUE DATE: _____

MODULE ONE - ESSAY WRITING ASSIGNMENT

Write a 5-paragraph essay explaining the three most important components of self-regulated learning and how these components can help students be more successful in their academic endeavors.

Rules:
1. 3 Full Pages, typed, double spaced.
2. No first person singular.
3. No plagiarism.
4. Begin introduction with a quotation, statistic, or anecdote.
5. Thesis must be last sentence of introduction.
6. Each body paragraph must have at least two sources. Only one source can be a direct quotation. The other in-text source can be paraphrase, summary, indirect quotation.

DUE DATE: _____

Chapter References

Dembo, M. H., & Seli, H. (2008). *Motivation and Learning Strategies for College Success: A Self-Management Approach*. 2nd. Edition. London.
Zimmerman, B., Bonner, S., & Kovach, R. (1996). *Developing self-regulated learners*. Washington, DC

Writing Module Two
The Classification Essay

In this chapter we will explore the mode of rhetoric that divides and defines. Think of the topic as a pie and you need to cut into equal pieces and then show why you divided it that way.

| Fall clothes | Winter clothes |
| Summer clothes | Spring clothes |

The pie above seems like a simple way to define different types of clothes by the time they are worn. These four divisions, however, do not fit well in the traditional five-paragraph essay which calls for three body paragraphs. How could we change this diagram and divide clothes into three categories?

Now we can have three body paragraphs and the scheme we have chosen does not overlap. What do I mean by overlap? Well, let's do the same paper and talk about three types of clothing: winter, summer and shoes. Well in this example there is overlap. Shoes belong in both summer and winter categories. You can NOT have overlap. Each of the groups needs to be mutually exclusive. Therefore, it is essential that you check to make sure you have a solid scheme and that there is no overlap before you start writing the paper.

Schemes (Principle of classification)

The scheme is the quality that sorts your topic into three distinct groups (or more). It is the organizing principle. It therefore needs to be your first thought when embarking upon a classification. Once you have the scheme, your classification will take care of itself. The scheme must be significant or people will not learn from your classification. An example of a trivial scheme is to classify children by nose size. Yes, it can be done, but what do you hope to understand from the classification? If I were grading it, I would say that something stinks about the paper.

Some effective schemes might be: age, size, duration, intensity, color, craft, level, shape, or purpose. Choose one and one only when you start your classification. You should not classify students by age and size at the same time. You should start with something simple, so let's classify the hairstyles in class. The scheme I will use is by how cool they make people look.

The first group is the conservative cuts. These make look people look the least cool.

The second group is the stylish cuts. These people look cool in a fashion-savvy way and stay within established realms.

The third group is the wild cuts. These people look cool and push their hair beyond "acceptable"; their coolness is unquestioned.

I could have done this same classification using length of hair, but what do I learn of people by hair length? Is it really interesting? I could interview people about their hair and how it represents them. I could find out why they chose their style and get information that might be interesting to the class. Do you think the same information would be available for hair length?

IN-CLASS EXERCISE

Classify people in your classroom by their work, their ambitions, their majors, or their attitude. See if you can narrow the broad scheme and find an interesting angle. For example, take attitude and narrow it to "attitude by interest intensity in English Comp" Why is this interesting? Well instructors are always fascinated as to why people take their classes!

TOPIC: PEOPLE IN THE CLASS

Scheme 1: Work

Narrowed Scheme:

Three Groups:

Scheme 2: Ambitions

Narrowed Scheme:

Three Groups:

Scheme 3: Majors

Narrowed Scheme:

Three Groups:

Scheme 4: Attitudes

Narrowed Scheme:

Three Groups:

GROUPS

Get into groups and share your classification principles and groups. Help each other refine the groups. Note the overlap between your ideas – did someone else express the same idea that you had in a better way? Did you articulate your groupings in a clear way that everyone else liked? It is important to notice what is common in ideas because collaboration pushes you to higher levels. Also, it should make you question the interest-level of your content – was your idea overly obvious? Is that why three others in the group had the same groupings?

ESSAY COMPONENTS IN CLASSIFICATION ESSAYS

THESIS STATEMENTS AND TOPIC SENTENCES

Just as you learned in the early chapter, every essay needs a thesis statement, and a classification essay needs a classification thesis. That means that the thesis should not only indicate the topic but also the mode (classification) of the essay. In this way, the writer is very clear on the purpose of the essay.

Example Thesis Statements
Read the sample thesis statements below and identify the topic, the three categories, and any words that indicate classification.

1. *When it comes to deciding how to cast their vote, voters fall into one of three types; those that vote based on the issues, those that vote based on the candidate's personality, and those that vote with the crowd.*

2. *Even though there is such a variety, parents can be divided into those who are autocratic, those who are democratic, and those who are permissive.*

3. *People all over America responded in different ways to Hurricane Katrina, participating in large-scale, small-scale, or hand-wringing aid efforts.*

THESIS PRACTICE

Using the exercise above in which you classified the class using different principles, write a thesis statement for each of those groups. Remember, you have already done the classification itself; now you put it into an academic thesis statement.

Work

Ambitions

_____

_____

Majors

_____

_____

Attitude

_____

_____

REVIEW

Exchange your thesis statements with a peer and check that they do the following:

1. Include the subject being classified.
2. Include the three groups.
3. Include word(s) indicating the rhetorical mode (classification).

THESIS STATEMENT EXPANSION

Now, you will write thesis statements on topics that you have not yet discussed. From the list below, choose three topics and write classification thesis statements for each one.

1. Responses to a disaster
2. Wal-Mart Shoppers
3. Television crime shows
4. Environmentalists
5. Divorces
6. Relatives
7. Famous cities
8. Facebook Users

Topic:

_____

_____

Peer Revision: (this is part of the review - do it later)

_____

_____

Topic:

_____

_____

Peer Revision: (this is part of the review - do it later)

_____

_____

Topic:

_____

_____

Peer Revision: (this is part of the review - do it later)

_____

_____

REVIEW

STEP ONE

Exchange your thesis statements with a peer and check that they do the following:
1. Include the subject being classified.
2. Include the three groups.
3. Include word(s) indicating the rhetorical mode (classification).

STEP TWO

Rewrite the thesis where necessary making it stronger and more effective. Rewrite it in the space provided.

TOPIC SENTENCES

You should also remember that every paragraph begins with a topic sentence. Coherence between paragraphs is an important part of essays. The topic sentences of your body paragraphs are tied directly to your thesis statement and the essay mode. Just as you include the overall essay topic, the sub-topic, and the mode in the thesis, so too do you include these things in the topic sentence. Look at the sample thesis from earlier:

EXAMPLE ONE - LEVEL ONE

THESIS: *When it comes to deciding how to cast their vote, voters fall into one of three types; those that vote based on the issues, those that vote based on the candidate's personality, and those that vote with the crowd.*

Topic Sentence Body Paragraph One:
The first type of voter selects a candidate based on that candidate's position on an issue.

Topic Sentence Body Paragraph Two:
The second type of voter selects a candidate based on that candidate's personality.

Topic Sentence Body Paragraph Three:
The final type of voter selects a candidate based on the crowd.

These topic sentences are fine and they do the work of a topic sentence. They have the key components and quite frankly, that makes them work. The question that you as a writer must ask is, can you do better? Look at the following two examples of transitions and topic sentences and discuss what makes them different from the first and from each other. Which do you prefer?

EXAMPLE TWO - LEVEL TWO

THESIS: *When it comes to deciding how to cast their vote, voters fall into one of three types; those that vote based on the issues, those that vote based on the candidate's personality, and those that vote with the crowd.*

Topic Sentence Body Paragraph One:
The first type of voter selects a candidate based on that candidate's position on an issue.

Topic Sentence Body Paragraph Two:
Another type of voter chooses a candidate on the basis of that candidate's personality.

Topic Sentence Body Paragraph Three:
The final voter from this group is less interested in the candidate's positions or personality and more interested in the crowd's opinion of the candidate.

EXAMPLE THREE - LEVEL THREE
THESIS: When it comes to deciding how to cast their vote, voters fall into one of three types; those that vote based on the issues, those that vote based on the candidate's personality, and those that vote with the crowd.

Topic Sentence Body Paragraph One:
One group of voters base their choice on the political candidate's position on an issue.

Topic Sentence Body Paragraph Two:
While issues may be significant to one voter group, another group of voters focuses on the political candidates personality.

Topic Sentence Body Paragraph Three:
Issues and personality do not interest the final group of voters as they are followers who base their vote on mass opinion of the political candidate.

TOPIC SENTENCE EXERCISE
Using the given sample topic sentences from earlier, write transitions and topic sentences for each of the three body paragraphs. Remember, the sub-points are there, so this really is an exercises on connecting the opening of a paragraph with the rest of your essay.

THESIS: Even though there is such a variety, parents can be divided into those who are autocratic, those who are democratic, and those who are permissive.

Topic Sentence Body Paragraph One:

_____

_____

Topic Sentence Body Paragraph Two:

_____

_____

Topic Sentence Body Paragraph Three:

_____

_____

TOPIC SENTENCE EXERCISE STUDENT VERSION 2 - STEP UP THOSE TRANSITIONS!

THESIS: *Even though there is such a variety, parents can be divided into those who are autocratic, those who are democratic, and those who are permissive.*

Topic Sentence Body Paragraph One:

_____

_____

Topic Sentence Body Paragraph Two:

_____

_____

Topic Sentence Body Paragraph Three:

_____

_____

PEER REVIEW
Exchange textbooks (emails or whatever format you are using) with a colleague and review the "before" and "after" sentences. Answer the following questions and then return the textbook to the author.
1. Did the sentences change? Yes/No
2. Did the transitions change? Yes/No
3. Did the sentence structure change? Yes/No
4. Did the sentences get better? Yes/No
5. Other comments:

REFLECTION

Read your colleague's comments. Review the sentences if necessary. Ask your colleague any questions that you need to.

TOPIC SENTENCE EXERCISE (Just one more)

Using the given sample topic sentences from earlier, write transitions and topic sentences for each of the three body paragraphs. Remember, the sub-points are there, so this really is an exercises on connecting the opening of a paragraph with the rest of your essay. WARNING: there is no re-write on this one, so strive for the best English, grammar, and coherence you can.

THESIS: *People all over America responded in different ways to Hurricane Katrina, participating in large-scale, small-scale, or hand-wringing aid effort*

Topic Sentence Body Paragraph One:

_____

_____

Topic Sentence Body Paragraph Two:

_____

_____

Topic Sentence Body Paragraph Three:

_____

_____

PEER REVIEW

Exchange textbooks (emails or whatever format you are using) with a colleague and review the "before" and "after" sentences. Answer the following questions and then return the textbook to the author.

On a scale of 1(weakest) to 5(strongest), how many points would you give each transition and topic sentence.

Topic Sentence One:
Topi Sentence Two:
Topic Sentence Three:
Explain your scoring:

REFLECTION: Read your colleague's comments. Review the sentences if necessary. Ask your colleague any questions that you need to.

A FINAL NOTE

Do not underestimate the value of these transitions and topic sentences. By writing a clear sentence at the beginning of each paragraph, you are showing that you are in control of the topic. You remind the reader at the beginning of each paragraph of the key points and the mode and as a writer, you remind yourself of that, too. Sometimes, that simple sentence can keep you on topic. In any essay you write, once you have your explicit thesis, you can write the opening to each body paragraph. The essay is almost writing itself. Well, okay, that's not true, but this is an important element of structure and as you will see in the other writing modules, the concept is constant; it is only the words and modes that change.

EMAIL OR WEB SPECIAL

Pair up **in class** and then email your partner three pictures that you believe have a similar theme but are different. For example you could send three pictures of celebrities on the red carpet, or three pictures of dairy farms of different sizes.

STUDENT A: Email your partner three pictures
STUDENT B: Email your partner three pictures

STUDENT A: Once you receive the pictures, you must write an explicit thesis statement that covers the first three pictures. Write the thesis here:

THESIS: _____

_____

You must then add two more pictures to each category. Bring everything to class.

Example: Your partner sends you pictures of Oscar Night dresses. Let's say you divide the three Oscar dress pictures into elegant, risqué and odd. You have your groups.

Then, you find two more pictures for each group. So for elegant, you have three pictures, for risque, you have three pictures, and for odd, you have three pictures and you bring all these pictures to class (if this is an online class post them in the correct forum). Your instructor may request they be printed or put into a digital format for presentation.

STUDENT B: Once you receive the pictures, you must write an explicit thesis statement that covers the first three pictures. Write the thesis here:

THESIS: _____

_____

You must then add two more pictures to each category. Bring everything to class.

Example: Your partner sends you pictures of Oscar Night dresses. Let's say you divide the three Oscar dress pictures into elegant, risqué and odd. You have your groups.

Then, you find two more pictures for each group. So for elegant, you have three pictures, for risque, you have three pictures, and for odd, you have three pictures and you bring all these pictures to class (if this is an online class post them in the correct forum). Your instructor may request they be printed or put into a digital format for presentation.

IN CLASS
In class, you will share your classification groups. You must be prepared for questions about your scheme and whether there is any overlap in your content. Can risqué be odd too? Oops. Maybe I should go with elegant, beautifully risqué and ugly.

This is the kind of exploration that can only be done with solid examples.Solid examples are what help you to see the value of being clear and of using solid examples.

WRITING MODULE TWO - CLASSIFICATION PRACTICE

Using the thesis you wrote above in the Web exercise, write a paragraph of about 450 words developing it. Use specific examples to support your points.

PLEASE READ
This can be a very difficult exercise because students tend to want to write an example paper. Three examples of questions, instead of three types of questions is a common mistake. There are three examples of Oscar dresses rather than three types of dresses. If you can't start your body paragraphs with the sentence One type, or One category – you might be in the middle of a paper that doesn't really classify. The first obligation of this text is to present ample examples to get you started. The

obligation of the student is to work until you understand the assignment. Don't write a full essay without a complete understanding of what your goal is.

PARAGRAPH VERSUS ESSAY REVIEW

As you already know (if you don't, go to Appendix) the essential difference between an essay and a paragraph is content (length and depth of analysis). Whereas a paragraph opens with a topic sentence indicating the three sub-points, an essay opens with an introduction at the end of which is a thesis indicating the three sub-points. Therefore, the thesis statement for an essay could be the topic sentence for a one-paragraph analysis. The topic sentence (with transition) for Body Paragraph One in an essay could be the transition sentence with supporting idea one in a paragraph. Similarly, the topic sentence with transition for Body Paragraph Two in an essay could be the transition sentence with supporting idea two in a paragraph. Do you see the connection? Do you see the similarity?

What does this mean for you right now? Well, you were asked to write a thesis statement. Now you are being asked to write a paragraph. Paragraphs don't contain thesis statements, so what do you do? Make your thesis statement the topic sentence of your paragraph. Easy, right? Below is a classification paragraph outline. This will help you stay within a paragraph format.

Classification Paragraph Outline

Topic Sentence: _____
_____

Transition + SP 1 (Group 1): _____
_____

    Details:

Transition + SP 2 (Group 2): _____
_____

    Details:

Transition + SP 3 (Group 3): _____
_____

    Details:

Concluding Sentence _____
_____

ANALYSIS OF REAL-WORLD EXAMPLES

The following is an example of an essay. The assignment was to classify voters. There are instructor comments in parenthesis.

Gore Vidal said: "Half of the American people have never read a newspaper. Half never voted for President. One hopes it is the same half." (good opening quote) This statement points to one of the biggest problems with the American voter, a lack of knowledge about the issues and candidates. When it comes to deciding how to cast their vote voters fall into one of three types; those that vote based on the issues, those that vote based on the candidate's personality, and those that vote with the crowd. (might the crowd voters not overlap with the personality voters? Otherwise a clear thesis)

The first type of voter selects a candidate based on that candidate's position on an issue. (good topic sentence) This voter usually feels very strongly about one particular issue and looks to the candidate who supports their view. An issue that has always polarized issue voters is that of abortion. In his article regarding one-issue politics John Piper shows how strongly a voter can feel about the issue when he states that a person that endorses the right to kill unborn children should never be allowed to hold office. In the 2008 Presidential election an example of this type of voter would be a voter that feels strongly about ending the war in Iraq. This person would be more likely to vote with a democrat. The BBC News Election Issues Guide compares the candidates on the issue of the war in Iraq. Hillary Clinton is for the phased redeployment and the end of the surge strategy; while Barak Obama backs a phased withdrawal of troops. (this says little about the how the voters see them) ~~On the opposite side all three republican candidates support the war and the continuation of a military presence in Iraq for as long as it takes.~~ *Another type of issue voter would be the farmer who cares about issues that affect the farm such as climate changes and the environment. The farmer would be more likely to vote for a candidate that strongly supports clean energy. (give specific support, quote a farmer if you want to use this* example) *The unfortunate thing about issue voters is that they may not look beyond the one issue that is the most important to them.* <u>The issue voter may find that they have voted for someone that they do not agree with on most issues.</u> *To make a wise choice, one must look at all the issues and find a candidate that agrees with the majority of them.*

The personality voter castes their vote based on the charisma and personality of the candidates. (there is some repetition here.) This voter tends to be a more emotional voter, often feeling a strong like or dislike for particular candidates. **John Kennedy, as the first president of the television age, utilized his personality to great advantage against his opponent Richard Nixon and won the election easily.** *Erika Tyner Allen describes how during the 1960 Kennedy-Nixon Presidential debates, people that just listened rated Nixon as having done better than Kennedy. Those that watched the televised debates overwhelming rated Kennedy as having won. According to Jill Lawrence of USA Today, during the first months of the 2008 primary election many people felt that Hilary Clinton not only lacked personality but that she was "chilly." (do they not still vote for her?) This rush to judgment hurt Hilary in the polls even though her campaign strategists immediately responded by making Hilary more approachable. The more charismatic the candidate the more likely they are to appeal to the personality voter* <u>however, personality does not a President make</u>. *Voters of this type may be terribly disappointed in their candidate's performance once in office as they did not understand where the candidate stood on the issues. Making an informed decision is always a better decision.*

The last type of voter is the voter that votes with the "crowd." (clear topic sentence again.) The crowd voter relies on the opinions of others to decide how to caste their vote. A celebrity endorsement appeals to this kind of voter. When Oprah Winfrey gave her endorsement to Barak Obama, she took many of the crowd voters to his camp. Obama's ratings in the polls went up immediately. (give exact numbers here, this is the place for research) On his bloggingstocks site, Tom Barlow notes that Oprah's support tends to lend legitimacy to Obama's prospects. More recently Senator Edward Kennedy has joined the Obama camp. As reported by Washingtonpost.com reporters Anne E. Kornblut and Shailagh Murray, Senator Kennedy indicated that he felt that Obama has extraordinary gifts of leadership and character. This endorsement gives Obama a big boost in the polls just before the "Super Tuesday" primaries. (did it help him win the Mass.?) Crowd voters keep a close eye on the polls, changing their opinions based on the latest results. This voter is strongly influenced by their family and associates many times asking them their opinions on candidates and issues. They may also vote straight down their party lines, thus depending on the party to make their decision for them. (find a stat on how many voters always vote for their party regardless of candidate.) Crowd voters lack an opinion of their own, therefore not feeling any responsibility for their vote. They may end up feeling disappointed in the end, but will blame someone else for that disappointment.

Three different types of voters, those that vote by issues, those that vote based on personality and those that vote based on the "crowd", three different approaches to the selection of a candidate, none of them good on their own. A good democracy not only requires participation, it requires informed participation. Plato said: "One of the penalties for refusing to participate in politics is that you end up being governed by your inferiors." No matter what voter type, voting without knowledge is a waste of a vote. To make an informed decision each voter must research the issues involved, research the candidates to establish how they stand on the issues and talk to people whose opinions they respect. Once all the information has been gathered then one can make an informed decision. Make a difference, don't just vote, vote with knowledge.

ANALYSIS

Now that you have read the sample essay, read it again and identify the following parts.

- ❖ Thesis Statement
- ❖ The three groups of voters
- ❖ Body Paragraph One Topic Sentence
- ❖ Support used
- ❖ Body Paragraph Two Topic Sentence
- ❖ Support used

- ❖ Body Paragraph Three Topic Sentence
- ❖ Support used
- ❖ Conclusion

IN-CLASS EXERCISE

Share your analysis with a partner or group. What observations do you have that are similar and what do you have that are different? Share your impressions on the quality of the content as well. If you have any areas of uncertainty or disagreement, ask your professor.

REAL-WORLD SAMPLE TWO

This essay was in response to the prompt to classify responses to a disaster. The Works Cited Page at the end is not part of our analysis, so don't worry about that or its flaws. This essay does not contain any instructor's comments. Read the essay and then complete the analysis that follows.

"Government failed because it did not learn from past experiences, or because lessons thought to be learned were somehow not implemented. If 9/11 was a failure of imagination then Katrina was a failure of initiative. It was a failure of leadership" (United States Congress). This was the grim conclusion drawn by a bipartisan congressional committee charged with researching the performance of government agencies in managing and executing the response to Hurricane Katrina. Time and time again government leadership has responded in an inept manner to disasters, therefore it is time for leaders from sectors other than government to rise up and take charge of disaster relief. American leaders, from all sectors, who have excelled in managing disaster responses, must learn to coordinate amongst themselves and stop relying on the government to direct response efforts. Hurricane Katrina killed over 1400 American citizens and destroyed over 120,000 homes, and when all was said and done it was the American government which stood alone as being responsible for contributing to the chaos instead of alleviating the pain of its citizenry. American leaders from all sectors must take the initiative to review the three types of responses to Hurricane Katrina, which consisted of ineffective government bungling, valuable private business innovation, and successful non-profit strategies, and determine the best and most effective line of attack to implement when the next disaster strikes the homeland shores.

Ineffective government bungling has always been a fact of life, but never before has the American government demonstrated its ineptness in taking care of business as clearly as during Hurricane Katrina. The incompetence ranged from mismanagement of funds, to outright fraud, and finally to a failure to deliver humanitarian services. A report issued by the Government Accountability Office (GAO) indicates that a substantial amount of funding intended to aid victims was used for services that did not directly relate to flood assistance. Journalist William Fisher pointed out some of the more egregious examples cited by the report which included money going towards "bail bonds, payment of prior traffic violations, tattoos, massage parlors and condoms" to mention just a few discretions. Numerous incidents of outright fraud were revealed in two separate reports; one by the GAO and the second by Homeland Security Department's office of inspector general. The GAO report to the Committee on Homeland Security cited several incidents including an overall estimate of contractor fraud. "Overall, we estimate that FEMA's ineffective management resulted in about $30 million in wasteful and improper or potentially fraudulent payments to the contractors from June 2006 through January 2007 and likely led to millions more in unnecessary spending beyond this period." Even worse than the government's inability to oversee funding was their failure to respond to the dire humanitarian needs of the people. It was definitively due to the lack of disaster response planning on the part of the government, as noted by journalist Peter Katel, that "in the days following the storm, New Orleans became an international symbol of government dysfunction. Tens of thousands of residents unable to evacuate clung to rooftops or flocked to the New Orleans Superdome, which was unequipped to receive them."

On the other hand, valuable private business innovation stands in stark contrast to ineffective government bungling. It was Jefferson Parish Sheriff Harry Lee who stated the obvious so succinctly, "If the federal government would have responded as quickly as Wal-Mart, we could have saved more lives." Sheriff Lee was right. In Barbaro and Gillis' article on Wal-Mart they reported that it was Wal-Mart's CEO, H. Lee Scott Jr. who called his executive team to task and told them clearly that he did not want a "measured response" to this disaster. In no uncertain terms he told his team, "I want us to respond in a way appropriate to our size and the impact we can have." And, respond they did – it was Wal-Mart who donated over "$20 million in cash, 1500 truckloads of free merchandise, food for 100,000 meals, and the promise of a job for every one of its displaced workers." If only the American government could have mustered the same response – lives would have been saved. The most outstanding examples of technology coming to the rescue were also from the private business sector; specifically from the geospatial companies based in the Mississippi area. Becky Gillette's reporting on this topic demonstrated how through the use of their innovative technology and quick implementation, when local run utilities failed, emergency responders used geospatial technology from private companies such as NVision Solutions Inc. to find victims of the hurricane, rescue them, and bring them to safe harbor.   In addition to the immediate response provided by the geospatial industry, other representatives of private industry pitched in as well. GMAC provided OnStar services for all of their customers located in the disaster area. The OnStar services which were made available included re-routing for customers who were travelling through the area, revising travel arrangements, and even offering to contact friends and families to assure them that their loved ones were safe and in good hands (B-A-W-B web site). All of these examples represent American ingenuity and compassion at its best.

One of the most important lessons learned from Hurricane Katrina is that the non-profit sector is just as capable as private business in providing successful strategies in times of crisis. It was the non-profit arm which reached out and answered the call during the disaster and remained in place to help the victims rebuild their lives. The rebuilding of the Gulf Coast's homes, neighborhoods, local services, business, and lives of its citizenry is just as important, if not more so, than the initial response to the disaster. This is the area where the successful non-profit strategies have operated in a manner which is worth noting and replication. One of the best examples of a successful non-profit response was from Catholic Charities. Journalist Matt Malone reported on Operation Helping Hands, a Catholic Charities relief agency, who made it their mission to help victims, whose homes had been damaged beyond repair, to salvage what they could of the contents and then gut their original homes. This is only the first step in recovery, but an important one nonetheless – and they aren't leaving until the job is done. An additional advantage to non-profits is that they are able to provide services and supplies to victims on an as-needed basis without burgeoning government bureaucracy slowing the process down. In Megan Reid's paper, "Survivor's Perceptions of Federal and Non-Governmental Responses to Hurricane Katrina", which included a survey of 71 Hurricane Katrina survivors conducted by the American Red Cross, "Several people remarked that the government was useless but that private organizations, particularly Red Cross and Catholic Charities, were helpful in a timely manner." In the United States Department of Homeland Security's report on the first year post Katrina, they cited that the Red Cross, working alongside the Southern Baptists, opened and managed 1400 shelters and provided services to over 1.5 million families in the immediate aftermath of Katrina. In a study conducted by the federal government the work of nonprofits was praised and several examples of successful strategies were cited. Some of those examples were: The Salvation Army who mobilized 178 canteen units and set up 11 field kitchens to serve more than 5.7 million hot meals, and 8.3 million sandwiches, snacks & drinks, and Habitat for Humanity who used its donations and pledges to begin construction or to complete nearly 400 homes, and it has placed more than 14,000 volunteers. By the summer of 2007, Habitat for Humanity planned to have built 1000 homes in the region.

It is obvious from the eyewitness observations, independent studies, and the government's own reports that many different agencies and individuals from many different sectors responded to the Hurricane Katrina disaster. It is just as obvious that some were more effective than others in answering both the immediate and long-term needs of the people who were directly affected by this catastrophe. It is clear, after studying and comparing the government's response, which ranged from mismanagement of funds, to outright fraud, and finally to a complete failure in delivering humanitarian services that the government is not the most effective agency when it comes to handling the needs of the people during or after such a disaster. However, it is apparent that private business and non-profits are capable of performing in an exemplary manner and are able to lead the way in providing exactly what the victims of devastating disasters need at exactly the right time. Therefore it is imperative that the lessons of Hurricane Katrina be learned before there is another disaster of similar proportions, as there is sure to be in the near future. American leaders from all sectors must first focus on keeping the ineffective government bunglers out of the response business and secondly on taking the initiative to put in place more resources to support the tried and true efforts of the valuable private business innovators, and successful non-profit strategists.

ANALYSIS - ON YOUR OWN

For the essay you just read, identify the following elements.
- ❖ Thesis Statement
- ❖ The three types of responses
- ❖ Body Paragraph One Transition and Topic Sentence
- ❖ Support used
  - ○ Examples
  - ○ In-text references (quotations, paraphrases, etc.)
- ❖ Body Paragraph Two Transition and Topic Sentence
- ❖ Support used
  - ○ Examples
  - ○ In-text references (quotations, paraphrases, etc.)

- ❖ Body Paragraph Three Transition and Topic Sentence
- ❖ Support used
  - ○ Examples
  - ○ In-text references (quotations, paraphrases, etc.)
- ❖ Conclusion Topic Sentence

ANALYSIS - PAIRS OR GROUPS

Compare your analysis with another student or another group of students. Did you miss anything? Together, answer the following questions:

1. What are the strengths of this essay?
2. What are the weaknesses of this essay?
3. Does the essay have clear structure?
4. Does the essay have sufficient supporting points for each paragraph?
5. What grade would you give this essay and why?

REAL-WORLD SAMPLE TWO

This essay was in response to the prompt to classify leaders. This essay does not contain any instructor's comments. Read the essay and then complete the analysis that follows.

Path to success of business Leaders

"Only through experiences of trial and suffering can the soul be strengthened, vision cleared, ambition inspired and success achieved"(Helen Keller). Having success in business requires hard working and dedicated professionals, who have the will to make sacrifices in order to become leaders. Business leaders have distinct paths to success some take the traditional paths while others take less traditional paths. Highly successful business leaders can be classified into three distinct groups based on their primary path to success: education, hard work, or inheritance.

The first group of business leaders is those who have inherited their family wealth and name. The reason why this group of business leaders is so distinct is because they were born wealthy which gave them financial security. For example, they have the advantage of going into prestigious universities such as Harvard Business, Princeton, and Yale. While attending these schools they have the opportunity to form well known connections and networks with people in high places, among their peers' and educators'. Most universities host experienced professors who teach real world experience advice, thus giving an insight in the business work-force. For instance, Donald Trump a well-known business leader inherited his families' wealth. "He entered Fordham University and then transferred to the Wharton School of Finance at the University of Pennsylvania from which he graduated in 1968 with a degree in economics."(biography.com) Trump had the advantage of furthering his career when he later joined his father's company, the Trump Organization. Donald J. Trump "is the definition of a success story, continually setting new standards while expanding his interests…He is the classic businessman – a deal-maker without equal and a passionate philanthropist."(investingvalue.com) Due to his success, Trump has continued to do well with expanding his business not only in his family's business, but in other fields such as: reality shows, talk shows, and radio stations. Another example, is when a family business is inherited those business leaders have the advantage of beginning their career with the family, enhancing their success to later expanding the family business. According to the *Encyclopedia of Business* family-owned businesses are recognized today as an important and distinct organization in the world economy. In *Forbes* study on the success of people born rich, its reports stated that the wealthiest businessmen demonstrate their success by being born wealthy. Due to their inheritance of family wealth and name, these groups of business leaders have an advantage of the path to success.

Another key group of leaders are those who pursue education as the basis of their success. The most traditional path to success for a business leader is his or her pursuit for education through different degrees. The educational path to success allows for the business leaders to gain "experience at post-secondary education, they have the opportunity to read books and listen to the lectures of top experts in their fields."(educationalpath.org). In order to become successful, business leaders need to attain a business degree. For many business leaders, education is a trusted path that leads them to success. In many instances of success education has been the leading cause for their motivation on how far they can achieve their goal. An example is to what extent a business leader pursues their degree while attending a university. The different degrees that most business leaders desire to pursue are; B.A. (business administration degree) in business and M.B.A (master's administration degree). In the process of obtaining those degrees, these leaders must apply for internships leading to a desired position in a business. As opposed to working in a small business and working their way the ladder to a higher position through their progression in business. Furthermore, people who are pursuing business opportunities take the route of going back to school to get educated and build a portfolio, which is essential when applying for internships. Getting an education also gives the business leaders a great cornerstone in the pursuit to their future. Obtaining a degree offers many advantages, some of them including a vast amount of career opportunities in a variety of job sectors, and well-paying jobs. In addition "The Business Administration graduate also benefits from a much larger pool of open positions that they can apply for, thus increasing their chances of landing a good job immediately after graduation without having to relocate."(www.lpn-to-rn.net). According to Harvard Business Law, business leaders approach the daunting task, called networking. They pursue business networking by *operational, personal,* and *strategic* ways. Furthermore, an educational path to success is an alternative path that business leaders can pursue when they do not have inheritance of family wealth and name.

Although some successes of business leaders comes from inheritance while others comes from education, the key and most important path to success can be achieved by hard-work. Many business leaders make the decision to pursue the less traditional route, in which they don't the financial support to go to a university. Also there are those business leaders who did pursue a university education, but needed to seek their passion in a different way. These business leaders are known as the "university drop-outs". For instance, Bill Gates was born into a family with parents who were comfortable professionals. He went to a private school first, and then went to Harvard University for better prospects. Although Bill Gates had the financial support to go to a prestigious university, "Gates left Harvard to devote his energies to Microsoft, a company he had begun in 1975 with his childhood friend Paul Allen."(Microsoft.com) With their business empire they transformed their childhood fascination with computers into a global empire. Another successful college drop-out who pursued business leadership through passion was Steve Jobs. After high school, Jobs enrolled at Reed College in Portland, Oregon but since he was lacking direction, he dropped out of college after six months and spent the next 18 months dropping in on creative classes. This successful business leader was a master at work; he was driven by a new idea and always was an intelligent and innovative thinker. Both innovators "Jobs and Wozniak were credited with revolutionizing the computer industry by democratizing the technology and making the machines smaller, cheaper, intuitive, and accessible to everyday consumers."(Harvard Business) These university dropouts were the "hard working type" but nonetheless they had the opportunity of going to a university, however they found their growth in business leadership through other ways. In contrast to the "college drop-out" hard workers, are the pure hard-workers who had no alternative but to pursue success in different ways. According to a CNN report by Paul Schmitz, they have found at Public Allies over the past two decades, over a thousand young adults without college degrees and have seen many achieve incredible success. This gives validity to the "pure-hard workers" who have succeeded without university degrees and have become Entrepreneurs. This group of hardworking leaders have pushed through the hard times, and successively achieved perfection. Furthermore, many business leaders got their starts without the benefit of degrees and have been successful.

Being successful in the business industry requires for the business leaders to pursue a path that will lead them to success. Although it may seem that only the wealthy are successful in the business field, due to their connections and family name it can be argued that this is not the case. With a lot of determination and hard-work a person can pursue their dreams and goals without having the advantage of a family name and wealth. Likewise, may it be through inheritance, education, or hard-work, business leaders must choose a path to success. Whether it may be through the traditional path of success in business leadership or the less traditional, one must have the self-determination to achieve the goal and succeed in the business world. Business Leaders come from all different "paths to success", the path chosen must be accomplished through perseverance and hard-work.

Works Cited

"Donald Trump." 2012. Biography.com 16 Jul 2012.

"Donald Trump." 2012. Biography.com 16 Jul 2012.Paul Schmitz. "Lessons from famous

college dropouts." *CNN Opinion*. CNN. 31 Dec. 2011.Web. 16 July 2012.

"Family-Owned Businesses". Reference for Business. Encyclopedia of Business, 2nd ed.

Web.

"Steve Jobs." 2012. Biography.com 20 Jul 2012.

Microsoft Corporation. Bill Gates: Chairman. *Microsoft*. 07 August 2011. 16 July 2012.

ANALYSIS - ON YOUR OWN

For the essay you just read, identify the following elements.

- ❖ Thesis Statement
- ❖ The three types of responses
- ❖ Body Paragraph One Transition and Topic Sentence
- ❖ Support used
  - ○ Examples
  - ○ In-text references (quotations, paraphrases, etc.)
- ❖ Body Paragraph Two Transition and Topic Sentence
- ❖ Support used
  - ○ Examples
  - ○ In-text references (quotations, paraphrases, etc.)
- ❖ Body Paragraph Three Transition and Topic Sentence
- ❖ Support used
  - ○ Examples
  - ○ In-text references (quotations, paraphrases, etc.)
- ❖ Conclusion Topic Sentence

ANALYSIS - PAIRS OR GROUPS

Compare your analysis with another student or another group of students. Did you miss anything? Together, answer the following questions:

1. What are the strengths of this essay?
2. What are the weaknesses of this essay?
3. Does the essay have clear structure?
4. Does the essay have sufficient supporting points for each paragraph?
5. What grade would you give this essay and why?

MODULE TWO - ESSAY WRITING ASSIGNMENT

Write a 5-paragraph essay classifying responses to a disaster.

Rules:

1. 3 Full Pages, typed, double spaced.
2. No first person singular.
3. No plagiarism.
4. Begin introduction with a quotation, statistic, or anecdote.
5. Thesis must be last sentence of introduction.
6. Each body paragraph must have at least two sources. Only one source can be a direct quotation. The other in-text source can be paraphrase, summary, indirect quotation.

DUE DATE: _____

OTHER POSSIBLE CLASSIFICATION ESSAY TOPICS

1. Classify community college students into three interesting and original groups.
2. Classify voters in the last general election.
3. Classify Walmart Shoppers
4. Classify America's friends

COMMON CLASSIFICATION PITFALLS (ROOKIE MISTAKES)

PITFALL ONE

Not naming your groups. This is part content and part grammar. Your thesis needs to be parallel. That means that if your first thing is an adjective, you shouldn't then switch to a noun. For example:

INCORRECT: *Parents can be divided into the interesting, the ones who are traditional, and crazy attitude parents.*
CORRECT: *Parents can be divided into interesting, traditional, and crazy.*

In addition to being grammatically parallel, giving your groups names will help provide shortcuts throughout your essay. For example:

Parents can be divided into three groups: the parents who are always giving their children what they want, the parents who never listen to their children, and the parents who are constantly negotiating with their children in the pursuit of fairness.

Imagine having to refer to these groups throughout your essay? Are you going to repeat those long clauses each time? Not only would that not be good style, it wouldn't be very efficient. Contrast that with this:

Parents can be divided according to their parenting styles into the autocrats, the democrats, and the permissives.

Now you have three simple terms that you can work with throughout a paper.

PITFALL TWO
Lack of support for the three classes is a common mistake. If you only have one person with a wild haircut, does that really make the classification relevant? Find groups that are populated by enough individuals that they are seem important. If everyone in class in highly motivated to take English Composition then my classification scheme needs to be modified. Make sure you have enough examples for each group, and that's what we'll work on next.

PITFALL THREE
Another hazard of classification is *overlapping* among the members of the class, that is, not making a sharp enough distinction among the members. If you classify types of dogs as mongrels, thoroughbreds, and house dogs, you have made a mistake. The third *category* is so large as to embrace the other two because both mongrels -and thoroughbreds can be house dogs also. You should seek another way to classify types of dogs. Yes, this was mentioned earlier, but it is still a common error and warrants being placed in here twice – just so you remember!

PITFALL FOUR
Another danger is setting up categories that lend themselves to *simplistic treatment.* If you classify dogs as long-haired, medium-haired, and short-haired, you have made a rather nonproductive distinction among types of dogs. This classification lends itself only to a discussion of hair length, the results of which will not be particularly profound or informative. Yes, this was touched on earlier, too, but it is still a common error and warrants being reinforced!

WRITING BREAK 4
Using Examples

Examples are possibly the most useful and definitely one of the most common forms of oral and written discourse. Ask a friend what he/she means and nine times out of ten, the friend will answer with an illustration, an example.

When doing this example essay, the most common question I hear is "How many examples do I need?"

The answer to this question is simple – enough examples to make your point and make it well.

Of course this leads to another question - "In what order should I put my examples?"

Of course, you aren't going to like the answer...

No one pattern will work all the time, and it's going to depend on the point that you are making. Remember, the essay is not a list of examples. The essay is an idea which you are supporting through examples. Do you see the difference? You also need to decide when you have used enough examples or exhausted one example and need a new one.

If you're trying to define what it means to be a good teacher, how many examples of good teaching do you have to give before you make your point?

- ❖ You need enough examples to make a valid point
- ❖ You don't want so many that your reader will put down the essay and walk out the door.

Essentially, examples can be categorized in the following ways:
- ❖ Lists
- ❖ Short examples
- ❖ Extended examples

Lists

Television can be a great source of education and information. For the younger viewer, there are many educational programs on television, especially on PBS Kids. Such programs include Sesame Street, Caillou, Barney, and Dora the Explorer. For the older viewers, The Learning Channel provides programs on home improvement such as Trading Spaces, In a Fix, and Trading Rooms.

Short Examples

Television can be a great source of education and information. For the younger viewer, there are many educational programs on television, especially on PBS Kids. One famous example is Sesame Street which teaches the alphabet and numbers using Muppets and famous guests. . For the older viewers, The Learning Channel provides educational programming on home improvements. One successful show is Trading Spaces in which two families swap rooms for two days and designers renovate the rooms.

Extended Examples

Television can be a great source of education and information. For the younger viewer, there are many educational programs on television, especially on PBS Kids. One famous example is Sesame Street which teaches the alphabet, numbers, and life lessons using Muppets and famous guests. Last week, for example, Julia Roberts was on the show with the furry cute monster Elmo. Elmo was trying to make Julia afraid but Julia kept laughing because she didn't find Elmo scary. When Elmo got upset, Julia acted scared and ran away. This made Elmo very proud but then Julia came back and scared him and he learned that being afraid wasn't actually much fun. He also learned that just because he was a monster, he didn't need to make others afraid. For the older viewers, The Learning Channel provides educational programming on home improvements. One successful show is Trading Spaces in which two families swap rooms for two days and designers renovate the rooms. In one episode set in Los Angeles, one family (Family A) redesigned the other family's (Family B) living room and Family B redesigned Family A's bedroom. The designers and builder showed viewers how to take an old coffee table and make it into a new end table by sanding it down and then varnishing the wood. They also added new metal legs to the table top to make it seem more modern.

Finding good examples in an essay is always a challenge whatever the style of essay. Here is a practice exercise for you to work on finding appropriate examples. This is a paragraph classifying parenting styles. The information defining the characteristics is there for you. What is missing from the paragraph are the specific examples for each group of parents. With a partner, work to create a strong example that will not only illustrate the group under discussion but will illustrate it in such a way that the reader will have a clear and full understanding of that particular group of parents.

Since the word 'parents' encompasses such a large number of people, it is easy to understand why there are so many types. Even though there is such a variety, parents can be divided into those who are autocratic, those who are democratic, and those who are permissive. The autocratic parents' words are the law, and when they say jump, everybody must do so. These parents assume that they know what is best for their children and that they will learn discipline and respect for authority from such regimentation. The perfect example....... Not quite so strict as the autocratic parents are the democratic parents. These parents are willing to discuss rules and punishments with the children and to listen to their side of an argument. Instead of laying down so many iron-clad rules, the democratic parents work as advisors because they realize there are some facts about life that children must learn on their own. For example..............Moving along the scale of strictness from the autocratic past the democratic stands the next group of parents: the permissive parents. In this household, there are no rules and little guidance. Frequently, these parents are too busy to take *time* with their children and leave their rearing to television, school, and, perhaps, chance. Although these parents' *children* seem to "have it made," they really suffer a disadvantage not even the autocrats' children have. They have no concept of authority and in later life will have to make sharp adjustments to accommodate themselves to the rules that all adults must abide by. A clear example of this..........All three of these parental types are easily recognizable by their relationship with their children, but one, the *democratic,* stands out as the most admirable type.

You can do this individually or in pairs.

Example Autocratic Parents

Short:

Extended:

Example Democratic Parents:

Short:

Extended:

Example Permissive Parents

Short:

Extended:

GUESS THE GROUP

After completing your examples, each group will share one of their examples with the class. You must NOT tell which group you are exemplifying – the rest of the class must guess. If your example is effective, your colleagues will have no trouble identifying to which class it belongs.

WRITING MODULE THREE

The Cause or Effect Essay

It is the simplest and perhaps the first means of expressing your opinion in conflict with either a sibling or parent. Why? Because! Because why? Because because. You can see the mathematical progression of this argument and it can go as far as ten becauses in my case with a very persistent older sibling. This is a familiar mode of rhetoric, but don't underestimate the need for aggressive research. "Just because" is a very weak response, and it is one we fall back on when we haven't researched the topic enough. Even if you have strong ideas about why something is happening, you still need to find people, facts and people with facts to back you up.

CAUSE ESSAY

Because cause comes before effect, we start here.

Cause essays seek to define and support the reasons for something that has happened in the past, is happening now, or will happen in the future.

Reasons Hillary will eventually win the presidency – the main reasons for global warming – the causes of the California blackouts of 2002 - the popularity of Lady Gaga

---

ACTIVITY

To see how cause works, in groups brainstorm five reasons for two of the topics in the above list. Share your causes with the class and in doing so, use complete sentences using the cause markers from the terminology list below.

BASIC TERMINOLOGY

Terminology of Cause

this is because,
for the reason,
being that,
for,
in view of,
because of the fact,
seeing that,
as,
owing to,
due to,
in that
since,
because

Terminology of Effect

as a result,
therefore
in spite of,
consequently,
hence,
for this reason,
thus,
because of,
in consequence,
so that,
accordingly
consequently,
so much that,

You can use this list as a reference for later.

ELEMENTS OF CAUSE/EFFECT ESSAYS

The Cause Thesis

As you now know because this book keeps telling you, every essay needs a thesis statement, and a cause essay needs a cause thesis. That means that the thesis should not only indicate the topic but also the mode (cause) of the essay. In this way, the writer is very clear on the purpose of the essay. In this mode of rhetoric (cause essay) we want an explicit thesis that defines three main reasons. Why three? Well, the five paragraph essay comes standard with three body paragraphs. The three body paragraphs should each illustrate one clear and unified argument for cause, and so three parts in the thesis lead directly into this model. (Remember the Writing Break earlier where this was explained?)

Example Thesis Statements
Read the sample thesis statements below and identify the topic, the three causes, and any words or phrases that indicate the mode (cause). Decide if each thesis is effective.

THESIS ONE

The primary causes of California's financial crisis are many.

THESIS TWO

There are three leading indicators for childhood obesity: lack of participation in sports, little understanding of nutrition, mass-produced junk food availability.

THESIS THREE

Immigration in the United States is an ongoing political issue because the number of illegal immigrants increases annually, because the government is afraid to tackle the issue with any real reform, and because Americans are typically sympathetic to the plight of many illegal immigrants.

TOPIC SENTENCES AND SUPPORT IN A CAUSE ESSAY.

You should also remember that every paragraph begins with a topic sentence. Coherence between paragraphs is an important part of essays. The topic sentences of your body paragraphs are tied directly to your thesis statement and the essay mode. Just as you include the overall essay topic, the sub-topic, and the mode in the thesis, so too do you include these things in the topic sentence. Look at the sample thesis from earlier:

Thesis: *There are three leading indicators for childhood obesity: lack of participation in sports, little understanding of nutrition, mass-produced junk food availability.*

Using the thesis above, it should be easy to construct topic sentences for each body paragraph.

EXAMPLE ONE

Topic Sentence Body Paragraph One:

One reason the youth of America is getting fat is the lack of participation in sports

Topic Sentence Body Paragraph Two:

Another reason our kids' waistline is bursting is that they haven't been taught about nutrition.

Topic Sentence Body Paragraph Three:

The final reason for the nation's childhood obesity problem lies with the manufacturers of junk food.

These topic sentences are fine and they do the work of a topic sentence. They have the key components and quite frankly, that makes them work. The question that you as a writer must ask is, can you do better? Look at the following two examples of transitions and topic sentences and discuss what makes them different from the first and from each other. Which do you prefer?

EXAMPLE TWO

Thesis: *There are three leading indicators for childhood obesity: lack of participation in sports, little understanding of nutrition, mass-produced junk food availability.*

Topic Sentence Body Paragraph One:
One important reason the youth of America is getting fat is the lack of participation in sports

Topic Sentence Body Paragraph Two:
Another key reason American children's waistlines are bursting is that they have not been taught about nutrition.

Topic Sentence Body Paragraph Three:
The most sinister cause of this nation's childhood obesity problem lies with the manufacturers of junk food.

EXAMPLE THREE

Thesis: *There are three leading indicators for childhood obesity: lack of participation in sports, little understanding of nutrition, mass-produced junk food availability.*

Topic Sentence Body Paragraph One:
One interesting reason the youth of America is getting fat is the lack of participation in sports

Topic Sentence Body Paragraph Two:
In addition to a lack of participation in sports is a lack of education about nutrition and this is a key factor in the youths' bursting waistlines.

Topic Sentence Body Paragraph Three:
While sports and nutrition are significant causes of obesity, the most sinister cause of the nation's childhood obesity problem lies with the manufacturers of junk food.

TOPIC SENTENCE EXERCISE

Using the given thesis from earlier, write transitions and topic sentences for each of the three body paragraphs. Remember, the sub-points are there, so this really is an exercises on connecting the opening of a paragraph with the rest of your essay.

THESIS: *Immigration in the United States is an ongoing political issue because the number of illegal immigrants increases annually, because the government is afraid to tackle the issue with any real reform, and because Americans are typically sympathetic to the plight of many illegal immigrants.*

Topic Sentence Body Paragraph One:

_____

_____

Topic Sentence Body Paragraph Two:

_____

_____

Topic Sentence Body Paragraph Three:

_____

_____

Now, the authors of this textbook have been instructors for a long time and we know that some of you will have done this exercise as well as possible and others will have done this exercise as quickly as possible and others will have done this exercise somewhere in between those two extremes. The authors of this textbook also know that the key to excellent writing is reviewing and re-writing, so take a look at those topic sentences and body paragraphs that you just wrote and see if you can do better - step up your writing game! You don't need to erase anything - there is space below for you to do this.

THESIS: *Immigration in the United States is an ongoing political issue because the number of illegal immigrants increases annually, because the government is afraid to tackle the issue with any real reform, and because Americans are typically sympathetic to the plight of many illegal immigrants.*

Topic Sentence Body Paragraph One:

_____

_____

Topic Sentence Body Paragraph Two:

_____

_____

Topic Sentence Body Paragraph Three:

_____

_____

PEER REVIEW
Exchange textbooks (emails or whatever format you are using) with a colleague and review the "before" and "after" sentences. Answer the following questions and then return the textbook to the author.

1. Did the sentences change? Yes/No
2. Did the transitions change? Yes/No
3. Did the sentence structure change? Yes/No
4. Did the sentences get better? Yes/No
5. Other comments:

REFLECTION
Read your colleague's comments. Review the sentences if necessary. Ask your colleague any questions that you need to.

> *Shallow men believe in luck. Strong*
>
> *men believe in cause and effect.*
>
> *Ralph Waldo Emerson*

EFFECTS

Effects are the same or are they?

It is interesting because causes and effects can be very closely related. Why a student takes a certain class might have the same causes and effects. They take the class because they are interested, they need it to graduate and it will help them get a job. The effect is that they are more interested, they can graduate and it helps them get a job.

Wow. So causes are almost the same as effects! Wait. There are times when they are totally different. The causes of the Iraq war and the effects of the Iraq war are very different. The causes of getting pregnant and the effects of a pregnancy hardly seem the same. So now we can say that cause is related to effect but not always the same. What happens before an event is not the same as what happens after as a result of an event.

Below are five different topics that could be developed into effect essays. Write EXPLICIT thesis statements for each topic then write topic sentences (first sentences) for each body paragraph. Remember to write transitions in those topic sentences as well, just as you did in the exercise earlier for the cause essay outlines.

Topic: The environment

Thesis statement:

Topic sentence 1:

Topic sentence 2:

Topic sentence 3:

Topic: Electric cars

Thesis statement:

Topic sentence 1:

Topic sentence 2:

Topic sentence 3:

Topic: Bad grades in an online class

Thesis statement:

Topic sentence 1:

Topic sentence 2:

Topic sentence 3:

Topic : Good grades in a regular class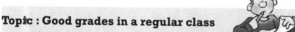

Thesis statement:

Topic sentence 1:

Topic sentence 2:

Topic sentence 3:

Topic: The election of Obama

Thesis statement:

Topic sentence 1

Topic sentence 2

Topic sentence 3

REFLECTION

Do you have any questions regarding thesis statements and topic sentences?

Are you seeing that these sentences are all essential and similar across mode?

Are you making those important connections?

Practice for Cause and Effect

Now that you have kind of grasped cause and effect, you are going to do an activity that will solidify your understanding of both and hopefully, help those of you who get confused within the language to really clarify which is which.

NEW APP HITS THE MARKET!

That is right. You are going to come up with a new app.

STEP ONE (paragraph one)
In groups, give your group a name and start figuring out how to come up with a new app and find at least five steps that you think will be necessary to bring your product to market.

STEP TWO (paragraph two)
Complete a mission statement. In your mission statement, give four reasons why this app will change the way that people do something.

Consider conducting some research into the field that you are entering; this will help you distinguish your product from the others. This separation from market competitors is a major reason your app will do well. Reasons require support, so do the research. It is difficult to compose a paragraph without sufficient support.

STEP THREE (paragraph three)
Now that everyone knows how to bring your app online and why the app will prosper, the next step is to predict what will happen once your app is launched. What will change? What profits will you see? Will those profits be immediate or long-term?

REAL-WORLD EXAMPLE 1

Getting a new app on to the market and making it successful is hard work but worth it if you have an app that is just sure to do well and catch on in today's society. Which is exactly what we have, to begin preparation on our police radar application and to eventually get the new app out in the market for distribution to consumers we will begin by contracting an established company by the name of radar shield technologies. It is then that we will attempt to partner up with this company and discuss mutual interest that will financially benefit both their company and ourselves, from this point the objective would lead to sharing information and starting the process of building our first prototype and making sure our code for the app will run efficiently with no bugs. We would then proceed by running numerous tests ran by our own employees; the next step would simply be reaching out to willing volunteers and determining candidates to test our product for a set period of time. After this trial we would finalize by asking the volunteers questions, about whether or not they had any questions or suggestions based on their experience with the app. Once the final adjustments are made and all tests have been completed the next phase of getting our product to market would begin. We would advertise our product through as many means we have available to us. Including magazines, online ads, newspapers, billboards, and television and or radio commercials. And then when the time comes that we are ready to release our app to the public we would do so by making it available in The Google Marketplace making it exclusive to Android devices a first and then moving on to make it compatible with iPhones and all other varieties of cellular devices.

There are many reasons for why our app would arouse people's interest and make them want to purchase the product but three clear reasons that I'm sure everyone could understand and relate to would be the convenience of it, it is more affordable and it would be a huge help in keeping their driving records clean. Our app is a hundred times more convenient than having a real police scanner; it's already installed into people's cell phones which they carry with them at all times anyways. It's not some big bulky machine they have to display in their car, it's in the phone, and people could use it while walking around if they wanted too. They don't necessarily have to be driving to get the benefits out of this simply amazing app. It's also a lot cheaper than the real thing, so when you think about it, it would actually be a whole lot smarter to just buy our app, it's affordable, nobody needs to know you have it and it works wherever you want it too rather than just working in a car. It will be greatly helpful in avoiding traffic, fix it, or any other type of tickets, which also saves some more money for the user. The scanning technology that the app brings to your phone lets you know whenever there is a policeman or highway patrol within a two mile radius of you. This allows the driver to slow to the speed limit without causing attention, put on their seatbelts, get off their phones, or stop any other type of activity that could cause a ticket. The app would also help both younger and or older drivers to keep their driving records clean. In the event that they forget or lose their phone and are forced to go about the day without our app and they get a speeding ticket or offense of any other kind it is highly likely that the cop would go easy on them since they have no prior tickets.

There are many effects that this app will cause among the people that are smart enough to invest just a few dollars in it. Just a few of those effects would be social media, a higher awareness among drivers, more concentration and a whole lot more relaxed drivers on the road all because of one little app that you can get on your cell phone. As for the aspect of social media, it greatly benefits us, the makers of the app and our partners while it greatly benefits the consumers, the people using it even more than it would benefit the manufacturers. A lot can be accomplished just by word of mouth, which will spread rapidly with our product, someone will have an interest in our app and decide to try it out and then finding how convenient it is they would either recommend using it or brag about it to someone they know by telling them how well it actually works and how they have avoided however many possible tickets since they started using our app. We also believe that it will raise people's awareness of the many possibilities that they could undergo while driving, and the consequences of irresponsible driving. A lot of people will also have fewer distractions while driving if they are using the app. They won't be forced to worry about how text book precise their driving is as long as it's not reckless driving, they won't have to look down every street corner and constantly scan their mirrors for police if they are in a rush and driving five minutes over the speed limit. They will feel more relaxed and at ease while driving which in our eyes would lead to better drivers and calmer streets, which we know would definitely be enjoyed by everyone.

REAL-WORLD EXAMPLE 2

To start off, to make 'MAKE THAT SH(r)T', first thing we need to do is find a "printing press". We would be our own workers and at first delivery processes would be made by us. What were most concerned about is finding a printer that will meet our demands and is able to print directly on fabric. Now that we know who, what, how well make our shirts and deliverys, next step is to begin making the app. The app's layouts, theme, buttons, its main attraction. Once the customer sets up an account with MTS, orders will be made easy and right to the point, once they're 5 step process and sizing is over, that MAKE THAT SH(r)T button will be pushed and automatically be started by us. Our next step is to make a buisness plan. To make our money calculations, individual prices, and because this is a 7 man team (lucky number) and if things really hit off as nicely as this sounds our fourth step is to get our loan . This being our own business we need exact numbers and enough to do things legally, to have exactly what we want and to be able to give the customers exactly what they want. We want to do things right the first time. Our last and final step would be to show Apple and expand.

This era is about expressing yourself. Showing what your about through clothing and all the accessories that come with it. Show your own customs and values on your personalized shirt. If you don't want a Tshirt don't settle, because our 7 man team is creative, experienced, and all have different personalities to put into your piece, shirts dont only have to be shirts. We can turn you t shirt piece of clothing into an accessory, purse, string backpack or even a dress. No matter what social class you come from make expressing yourself easy, important and beneficial. Get exactly what you want. From punk rock patches to that winning picture of your teammates on the back of your favorite colored shirts, keep your memories strong and have immediate gratification with our easy MAKE THAT SH(r)T app.

Not all T-shirts are as expensive as they seem. If you go to the store you can find a pack of 3 normal white T-shirts. They range from 10-12 dollars. This means that we would charge around a minimum of 5 dollars per shirt. We would charge for paint, maintenance, delivery and a little something for the strings, needles and measuring. Realistically our shirts will run from 15-35 dollars a shirt plus shipping and handling. The more material and paint needed the more will be charged. Most of our profit will be coming from our accessories. Because we need a full shirt to start your project, a lot of scraps will be leftover because not all the shirt will be needed. With the customer's permission, used shirts will be used for bags, socks, and everything that isnt being worn on your back. Luckily, a lot of donation stores tend to have sales go on where you can get a bag waist high for about 10 dollars. With everything folded right we can get about 30 shirts, thats a 34 cent shirt that we can charge 20 dollars for. Profit will be divided evenly and prices would be adjusted to meet the customers demand to our supply. We will have a secret logo placed inside to know where your product comes from. We will raise curiosity, and let the clothing do its own expansion.

CAUSE - EFFECT ESSAY TOPIC ACTIVITY
GROUNDHOG DAY
STEP ONE
This module's essay is based on the successful romantic comedy *Groundhog Day.* Therefore, step one in this process is to watch the movie. Your instructor might show it in class or might ask you to watch it at home. Follow your instructor's directions.

STEP TWO - FUN COMPREHENSION QUIZ - In the Appendix there is a
multiple choice quiz for students. This can be done in class as an activity, outside of class, alone, in groups - however it fits in to your schedule. Follow your instructor's directions.

STEP THREE - DISCUSSION QUESTIONS
These questions can be answered as you watch the movie or after you have watched the movie. There is overlap in these questions and in the multiple choice quiz questions in the quiz from Step Two, but that is deliberate and it is okay. There is reinforcement of basic content taking place.

These questions can be done as a carousel with students answering each section and then moving to the next section around the classroom. Each part can be posted on the board or on posters. They can also be done in small groups at desks or individually and then in groups for discussion. Follow your instructor's directions.

Questions

1. Who is he main character?

2. What is his job?

3. Who are the other two characters we meet and what are their jobs?

4. Where do the three characters go and why?

5. What do we learn about each of these characters in the short segment that you watched? Support your answers with specific examples.

6. What song is playing on the radio when Phil wakes up?

7. What day is it?

8.What do Phil's interactions with the following reveal about him and them?

Guy in hall

Mrs. Lancaster

Homeless man

Ned Ryerson

9.Does the groundhog see his shadow? What does it mean?

10.What tone does Phil use as he concludes his groundhog report?

11.How does Phil respond to the blizzard preventing him from returning him to Pittsburgh?

12.What does Phil do today that is different from the previous ones?

13.Map Phil's feelings throughout this segment.

14.How does this day end for Phil?

15.There is another change in Phil's attitude when he wakes up. Describe the change?

16.What does he do differently on this day?

17.How does he respond to Mrs. Lancaster, and Ned Ryerson?

18.How does he describe himself to Rita?

19.Rita quotes Sir Walter Scott: - What do you think she is trying to say?

The wretch, concentred all in self,
Living, shall forfeit fair renown,
And, doubly dying, shall go down
To the vile dust from whence he sprung,
Unwept, unhonored , and unsung.

20.Why did Phil talk to Nancy in the diner?

21.This Groundhog Day goes straight to Gobbler's Knob and Nancy. What does Phil do here?

22.How is Phil behaving now?

23.What is the surprising revelation at the end of this night when he is with Nancy?

24.This section opens with Phil on a wall narrating the events. How many days do you think it took to learn all of the events to this exact detail?

25.What is Phil's purpose? What does this show about Phil's character?

26.What does Phil do with the money?

27.Who is Phil's date at the movies?

28.How many times has Phil seen the movie? What does that imply?

29.This section starts with Phil talking to Rita. What does he ask her? How does he persuade her to have coffee?

30.What do you think is Phil's motivation in talking with Rita?

31.What qualities does Rita list as important in a man?

32.What does Phil do in this section to focus on Rita?

33.Why do you think Phil is spending so much time on learning about Rita and on getting Rita to respond to him?

34.Do you think that Rita believes Phil's character? Remember, she only experiences this day once.

35.How many groundhog days do you think this focus on Rita takes?

36.At the beginning of this section, the clock changes slowly and dramatically. Why?

37.How is Phil feeling in this section? Support your points.

38.In what tone is Phil's Groundhog Day report?

39.What is Phil's weather/winter prediction?

40.How many times does Phil destroy the clock?

41. In what tone is Phil's Groundhog Day report? What realization comes at the end of the report? What is the effect of this realization (what does Phil do?)? Make a causal chain for this section.

42. In what ways does Phil try to commit suicide?

43. What does Phil tell Rita that he is?

44. Why does Rita eventually believe that Phil is telling the truth?

45. What does Rita do to help Phil?

46. According to Phil, how long does it take to learn how to throw cards into a hat? What does this imply?

47. How is this different from the days that Phil and Rita spent together earlier in the movie?

48. How does this day end? Is there another Groundhog Day?

49. What is the first immediate difference about Phil in this section?

50. What activities do you see Phil engage in?

51. Why is Phil learning these things?

52. Who does Phil try to help? In what ways does Phil try to help?

53. What are the effects of Phil's help on Phil's attitude and emotional state?

54. What is Phil's focus from the beginning of this section on?

55. Who does Phil encounter and what are the relationships he has with these people

56. What effect does Phil's business and activity have on Rita?

57. What happens on the next Groundhog Day morning?

STEP FOUR - ANOTHER ANALYSIS

ANOTHER ANALYSIS

Phil's Journey

Break down the story in terms of Phil's feelings/mental state.

Stage One:

Stage Two:

and so forth

Support your stages with specific examples.

The portrayal of love in Groundhog Day

How is love portrayed in the movie.

Analyze and support.

Movie Themes

What are the major themes of the movie. Support each with specific examples.

CAUSE AND EFFECT SENTENCE WRITING PRACTICE

EFFECTS
Use complete sentences to answer the following questions.

What effect does being trapped in Groundhog Day have on Phil's professional performance?

What effect does being trapped in Groundhog Day have on Phil's social behavior and interactions?

What effect does being trapped in Groundhog Day have on Phil's philosophy of life?

CAUSES
Use complete sentences to answer the following questions.
What is the fundamental cause of Phil's predicament?

What are two key causes of Phil's ultimate transformation?

Why do schoolteachers use this movie to teach children lessons on behavior?

STEP FIVE - READING ACTIVITY (AND RESEARCH)

Below is an article from Ken Sanes at transparency.com. It provides some good ideas and thoughts. It also gets you talking about the movie. Moreover, it provides some good reading practice. Thus, you will read it (in class or out of class depending on your instructor's preference) and then we will talk about the key points from the article.

Groundhog Day: Breakthrough to the True Self
By Ken Sanes

An example of an exceptional work of moral fiction is the apparently minor comedy, Groundhog Day, which shows us a character who has to be exiled from normal life so he can discover that he is in exile from himself. In the movie, actor Bill Murray plays Phil, an arrogant, Scroogelike weather forecaster who spends the night in Punxsutawney, Pennsylvania, where he is to do a broadcast the next day about the annual ritual of the coming out of the groundhog. He wakes up the next morning, does his story and is annoyed to discover that he is trapped in Punxsutawney for a second night because of a snowstorm that comes in after the groundhog ceremony.

When he wakes up in his guest house room the next morning, lo and behold, it is the morning of the day before all over again. Everything that happened to him the previous day -- the man trying to start a conversation at the top of the stairs; the old high school acquaintance recognizing him on the street, the ritual of groundhog day -- it all happens again.

And, once again, due to inclement weather, he is forced to spend the night. When he wakes up the next morning, it is the same day as yesterday and the day before, with the same oncoming snowstorm keeping him stuck in town and the same events repeating themselves like a broken record.

And so it goes, day after day, as this misanthrope of a human being finds himself trapped in Punxsutawney on groundhog day in what science fiction would refer to as a time loop. If he does nothing different, events will repeat themselves as they were on the original day. But if he changes his behavior, people will respond to his new actions, opening up all kinds of possibilities for playing with the unfolding of events. Either way, with each "new" day, he alone remembers what happened in previous editions of the same day.

At first Murray's character responds with bewilderment. Then he despairs and begins to treat life as a game: he risks his life and gorges on food, expressing both his sense of hopelessness and his growing recognition that, no matter what he does, time will reset itself and he will wake up as if nothing had happened.

In one scene, which turns out to be central to the movie's theme, he expresses his despair to two working class drinking buddies in a local bar.

One of his two inebriated companions then points to a beer glass and sums up the way he is responding to his situation: "You know, some guys would look at this glass and they would say, you know, 'that glass is half empty'. Other guys'd say 'that glass is half full'. I bet you is (or I peg you as) a 'the glass is half empty' kind of guy. Am I right?"

But as the days pass endlessly into the same day, this half-empty character finally finds a purpose in life: learning everything he can about his female producer, Rita, played by Andie MacDowell, so he can pretend to be her ideal man and seduce her. When that fails, and his efforts net him slap after slap, day after day, his despair deepens and he begins to spend his days killing himself. He kidnaps the groundhog and drives over a ledge into a quarry; he takes a plugged-in toaster into the bath; and he jumps off a building, always waking up whole in the morning.

In desperation, he reveals his plight to the female producer and she stays with him (without sex), in his room, through the night. Once again, he wakes up alone in the same day.

But, enriched by this experience of intimacy, and by the fact that someone actually liked him for who he is, he finally figures out a constructive response -- he begins to live his life in the day allotted to him, or, rather, he begins to live the life he never lived before. Instead of allowing circumstances to impose themselves on him, he takes control of circumstances, aided by the fact that he has all the time in the world and the safety of knowing what will happen next.

He begins to take piano lessons from a music teacher who is continuously surprised at how proficient he is, since she always believes it is his first lesson. He learns how to be an ice sculptor, which is the perfect art form for him since everything he does will have melted away when he wakes up anyway. And he becomes more generous.

Then, an encounter with death -- an old vagrant dies in his day -- has a deep effect on him. At first, he can't accept the man's death and, in at least one subsequent edition of the day, he tries to be good to the old man, taking him out to eat (for a last meal) and trying, unsuccessfully, to keep him alive.

When he stops trying to force death to relent, his final defenses fall away and his compassion for the old man transfers to the living. He begins to use his knowledge of how the day will unfold to help people. Knowing that a child will always fall from a tree at a certain time, he makes it a point to be there and catch the child every time. Knowing that a man will choke on his meal, he is always at a nearby table in the restaurant to save him.

Slowly, he goes through a transformation. Having suffered himself, he is able to empathize with other people's suffering. Having been isolated from society, he becomes a local hero in Punxsutawney.

Now, he sees the glass as half full, and the day as a form of freedom. As he expresses it in a corny TV speech about the weather that he gives for the camera, at the umpteenth ceremony he has covered of the coming out of the groundhog:

"When Chekhov saw the long winter, he saw a winter bleak and dark and bereft of hope. Yet we know that winter is just another step in the cycle of life. But standing here among the people of Punxsutawney and basking in the of warmth of their hearths and hearts, I couldn't imagine a better fate than a long and lustrous winter."

In other words, having accepted the conditions of life and learned the pleasures afforded by human companionship, he is no longer like all those people who fear life's travails, and try to use the weather forecast, by human or groundhog, to control events. He accepts "winter" as an opportunity.

Finally, the female producer falls in love with the good person he has become and she again spends the night (although he falls asleep so, again, there is no sex.) They wake up in the morning. She is still there and it is the next day.

In a last bit of irony, the couple, (who get to know each other, in the Biblical sense, once the new day begins), decide to settle down in Punxsutawney. Like Maxwell Klinger in the last episode of MASH, Murray's character will end up living in the one place he couldn't wait to escape.

What is so powerful about Groundhog Day is the way it lets us experience what it would be like to make a breakthrough like this in our own lives. The movie shows us a character who is like the worst in ourselves. He is arrogant and sarcastic, absorbed in his own discomforts, without hope, and cut off from other people. Like us, he finds himself in an inexplicable situation, seemingly a plaything of fate. But, unlike us, he gets the luxury of being stuck in the same day until he gets it right. Whereas most of us go semi-automatically through most of our (very similar) days, he is forced to stop and treat each day like a world onto itself, and decide how to use it. In the end, he undergoes a breakthrough to a more authentic self in which intimacy, creativity and compassion come naturally - a self that was trapped inside him and that could only be freed by trapping him. Like many of the heroes of fiction, he can only escape his exile from himself by being exiled in a situation not of his choosing.

In telling this story, the movie hits on a message that is commonly found elsewhere and that appears to express an essential truth. When we get beyond denial and resentment over the conditions of life and death, and accept our situation, it tells us, then life ceases to be a problem and we can become authentic and compassionate. Murray's character makes two such breakthroughs: first he accepts being condemned to being stuck in the same day, then he accepts the fact that everyone else is condemned to die.

Inevitably, the movie also has mythic resonances and literary counterparts. Murray's character is like all kinds of saviors and heroes in well-known stories, secular and religious, who experience some combination of suffering and courage, until they go through a transformation to a new state of knowledge. Among the religious and mythic elements we can recognize in the story: he fights off his demons; he is changed by an encounter with death; he experiences a kind of rebirth; he appears to people to exist in time but he also exists outside of normal time; he manifests deep compassion; he is in the world but not of it, suffering with a special knowledge that he uses to save those around him; and he is given a second chance in life by the love of a beautiful woman. He condenses images of Buddha and the Beast, Scrooge and Jesus.

But the movie keeps myth and archetype, as well as message, blessedly in the background. It also employs only a little visual spectacle and only the barest minimum of fantasy, in the form of the ever-repeating day, to tell the story. It is effective because it is understated, allowing Murray and the theme to engage us.

Perhaps it gets a little too sweet as it moves toward a conclusion, but that is forgivable. At the end, it saves itself from going over the top by revealing that Murray's character still has some of the old, calculating, self inside him. As he and his new mate walk out of the guest house into the new, snow-covered day, he exclaims, with his new enthusiastic wonder at life: "Its so beautiful -- Lets live here."

Then, after the obligatory kiss, he adds: "We'll rent to start."

Happily-ever-after is very nice, the character slyly tells us. But in the real world it's important to keep your options open, just in case you need to beat a quick retreat.

DISCUSSION QUESTIONS
Answer the following questions and then discuss them in groups.

1. What is the main idea of this article?

2. Go through the article and identify its parts – where does it narrate? Where does it analyze? Mark notes or questions in the margins.

3. Find your favorite part of the article. Underline it. Explain why it resonates with you.

4. Is there anything in the article with which you disagree? Find it and explain.

5. The following is from the article. Paraphrase it. "In telling this story, the movie hits on a message that is commonly found elsewhere and that appears to express an essential truth. When we get beyond denial and resentment over the conditions of life and death, and accept our situation, it tells us, then life ceases to be a problem and we can become authentic and compassionate. Murray's character makes two such breakthroughs: first he accepts being condemned to being stuck in the same day, then he accepts the fact that everyone else is condemned to die."

STEP SIX - APPROACHING THE ESSAY

You have now done a lot of work on Groundhog Day - on understanding it beyond the immediate narrative. As you might have guessed, the essay in this unit is based on the movie. You actually have three choices but the movie forms the centre. The trick is to go beyond the movie in your research. For instance, if you are asked to write an essay on the following topic:

> Groundhog Day is a movie about change. Why does the protagonist fear change in his life?

GROUP ACTIVITY

This is not a difficult or tricky topic. However, you cannot write the whole essay using only Groundhog Day as your source, so what other areas of research could you tap into in the planning and writing of this essay? In a group, develop a research plan for the above topic. Complete the following as you do so:

ESSAY TOPIC:

ASSOCIATED TOPICS:

FOCUS OF ESSAY THAT MUST NOT BE FORGOTTEN:

BASED ON THE ABOVE:

    POTENTIAL INTERNET RESEARCH IDEAS:

        SEARCH TERMS

        SEARCH ENGINES

    POTENTIAL LIBRARY RESEARCH IDEAS:

    LIBRARY RESEARCH ASSISTANT:

STEP SEVEN
COMPLETE THE RESEARCH AND SHARE RESULTS

One of the easiest ways to disseminate the results is through a class website or wiki, but bringing printouts for classmates is also effective. When posting the results, it is not enough to just list what you found; you need to judge its usefulness (or potential usefulness) to the topic. You must also provide complete information so that everyone can access the resources you find.

REVIEW THE PROCESS AND REFLECT

One of the most fruitful activities you can do after this is to discuss the process of researching and judging the results. This can help you and your peers become more effective researchers and with that more effective writers. Consider the difficulties you had, the successes you had, and the surprises you had. Share those with each other. You will be surprised at the results.

NEXT STEP

You have now done lots of activities based around the movie, *Groundhog Day.* *At the end of this module, there is a list of essay topics based on this movie. You should be prepared now to handle any of those topics.*

Before you get there, there are some essays for you to analyze, just so you can remember the structure of the cause or effect essay.

ANALYSIS OF REAL-WORLD SAMPLE 1

Read the essay below and complete the analysis that follows.

Causes of High Energy Prices

"*The use of solar energy has not been opened up because the oil industry does not own the sun". -Ralph Nader. Industrialization has enabled economies to become more productive through the use energy. Gasoline, which is a form of energy produced from crude oil, gives life to many technologies and fuels most societies. The need for gasoline increases continuously; furthermore, the price of gasoline increases rapidly as well. Without gasoline, society and the everyday production that comes from it would come to a screeching halt. In recent years the price of gasoline has grown and is beginning to have an impact on society. The causes of high gasoline prices are an*

---

increasing demand, specific factors that ultimately create a dependency, and instability found within different economies.

High prices for gasoline are caused by a growing demand for the product. Supply and demand is an economic model describing effects on price and quantity in a market. When the amount of demand equals the amount of supply, an economy is in equilibrium; however, in recent years, due to specific reasons, the amount of gasoline demanded within economies is exceeding the amount supplied. Economic equilibrium is an important factor in keeping economies stable. A significant increase in demand results in a shortage of supply; therefore, to reach equilibrium, the price of the supply, which is gasoline in this case, will increase in hopes of calming the demand. In June of 2005 the U.S. Federal Trade Commission released a landmark study titled: "Gasoline Price Changes: The Dynamic of Supply, Demand and the Competition." To quote from the FTC's findings: "Worldwide supply, demand, and competition for crude oil are the most important factors in the national average price of gasoline in the U.S." and "The world price of crude oil is the most important factor in the price of gasoline. Over the last 20 years, changes in crude oil prices have explained 85 percent of the changes in the price of gasoline in the U.S." There are many causes for the increase in demand; for example, many economies are switching to an entirely industrial society, which results in the consumption of more resources, like gasoline. While the U.S. economy is expected to grow by an anemic 1.5 percent in 2008 and the prospects for Europe not much better, Tertzakian said developing economies in places like India and China are growing at an average rate of over 8 percent a year (CNNMoney). In 2008 the world was expected to use 1.4 million barrels more of oil per day compared to 2007, according to Lehman Brothers energy analyst James Crandell. Developing nations account for more than 1 million barrels of that growth (CNNMoney). Reasons for the increase in gasoline prices in the U.S. are result from low prices during the 1990s. Those low prices - partly caused by low gas taxes in the U.S. compared to other developed nations - both encouraged rapid consumption domestically (think SUVs) and under-investment in new production by the world's oil companies (BBC News). Another reason demand for gasoline increased in the U.S. has to do with the transportation sector. In 1950 the share of total US oil consumption attributable to the transportation sector was 54 percent. By 1970 it had risen to 56 percent, by 1980 it had jumped to 60 percent and by 1990 it had reached 67 percent. But it did not stop there. By 2001, 69 percent of US oil consumption was accounted for by the transportation sector as a whole (Rutledge 10). More than 50 percent of transportation in America reflects citizens with their own vehicles; therefore, this proves American citizens and their way of transportation is sharply increasing demand for gasoline, causing higher prices for the product.

Another reason gas prices are high is because specific factors create a dependency on the product. People have become so accustomed to personal transportation as opposed to public transportation, especially in the US, that they have no choice but pay for gas, no matter what the price. Also, gasoline is the main source of energy that keeps industrial societies, i.e. countries who progress through labor in factories and technology, together. Gasoline, which is made from crude oil, is so desirable that it has come to be thought of as a 'strategic' commodity; one without which no highly industrialized society can survive and whose availability must be guaranteed, if necessary, by military force (Rutledge 1). There are many reasons that justify why people are dependent on gasoline, but the sad truth is people have no options when it comes to buying gas; therefore, the product will be purchased regardless of the price. The United States imports over 60 percent of its oil from foreign countries and uses 20.4 million barrels of oil a day; therefore, they have little input in regards to the price of gas. Dependency is created through the fact that citizens have no say in terms of price; also, private gasoline stations have strict limitations on the price of their fuel, government subsidies and market competition create a set price. It's important to note that dependency on gasoline differs from dependency on other products. For example, meat can be considered a dependency, but the fact that meat can be produced in a free market, from a much wider variety of producers, and can be offered in different forms creates options; therefore, creating different prices and different choices. Gasoline has little options because top oil industries dominate the market and set the price. Also, new technologies that would serve in breaking away from this dependency, such as hybrid and hydrogen vehicles are being developed slowly and lack the ability to serve as a substitute to the combustion engine. It's also important to point out that though these new technologies do exist they remain very limited; for example, hydrogen cells can't be found around every corner in comparison to gasoline stations. Hybrid automobiles lack the versatility of combustion engines; furthermore, hybrid automobiles are more expensive, difficult and expensive to maintain, and don't solve the underlying issue because gasoline is still required for them to operate (Washington Post). OPEC, which holds two-thirds of the worlds oil reserves, has little incentive to increase production (BBC News). OPEC also sets limitations on oil exporters, which in turn limits the amount received by certain economies and increases the price. Gasoline has become the world's bloodline; there is no question that economies have become dependent on this product in order to function. Citizens of these particular economies also depend on gasoline; however, they not only pay for the price of crude oil, but also all other costs, including taxes imposed by their government.

High gasoline prices are caused by instability found within certain economies. Examples of instability in economies can be seen all over the world. The most basic principle of international relations states that all forms of government are striving for respect and power, meaning they don't want to be pushed around. Many foreign countries rely on exporting oil to world powers; therefore, peoples dependency on gasoline gives these countries power. Instability puts pressures on economies; these pressures disrupt normal supply output and result in higher prices. For example, In the past few years, Iran's Mahmoud Ahmadinejad, Russia's Vladimir Putin, and Venezuela's Hugo Chavez have all become more bellicose on the world stage-in some cases, seeking a bigger share of the profit from foreign oil firms or threatening to cut off oil supplies if attacked (BBC News). This example describes three unstable economies that are threatening to cut oil supplies; this threat puts pressure on the market and causes it to tighten up. "New supplies of oil from non-OPEC countries were supposed to come online in 2007 and ease some of these supply bottlenecks. But problems in Kazakhstan and Russia - as well as sweeping drilling bans in the United States - mean global consumption is growing twice as fast as non-OPEC production" (Verleger 29). These instabilities result in the continued reliance on OPEC oil and force countries to pay high gas prices. In 2006 increased tension in the Niger Delta region pushed up oil prices to more than $67 a barrel. Militants of the area quoted, "We will attack all oil companies, including Chevron facilities," it said. "Pipelines, loading points, export tankers, tank farms, refined petroleum depots, landing strips and residences of employees of these companies can expect to be attacked" (BBC News). This example shows some of the risks put on foreign refineries; these risks will ultimately result in higher gas prices because the product becomes difficult to produce. Instability found within the Middle-East accounts for many of the price surges in gasoline, but certain domestic issues regarding the U.S. have also had effects. The two most obvious cases of U.S. instability include the September 11th attacks and Hurricane Katrina. Both disasters created fear within the economy and both resulted in huge increases for the price of gasoline. Obvious examples of instability, such as the War in Iraq, create high gasoline prices, but it's also important to realize the impact smaller events, which are seen daily, have as well.

The world has become addicted to gasoline. Economies rely on gasoline to perform everyday tasks. The need for gasoline has become a major issue for many economies and is responsible for many conflicts throughout the world. The price of gasoline has significantly increased within the last decade and is starting to have serious impacts on society. The causes for high gas prices are an increased demand, uncontrollable dependency, and instability within certain economies. Gasoline and the crude oil from which it comes has become the most important resource for growing economies.

ANALYSIS

Now that you have read the sample essay, read it again and identify the following parts.

- ❖ Thesis Statement
- ❖ The three CAUSES
- ❖ Body Paragraph One Topic Sentence
- ❖ Support used
- ❖ References and style of reference (direct quotation, paraphrase)
- ❖ Body Paragraph Two Topic Sentence
- ❖ Support used
- ❖ Support used
- ❖ References and style of reference (direct quotation, paraphrase)
- ❖ Body Paragraph Three Topic Sentence
- ❖ Support used
- ❖ Support used
- ❖ References and style of reference (direct quotation, paraphrase)
- ❖ Conclusion

GROUP EXERCISE

Share your analysis with a partner or group. What observations do you have that are similar and what do you have that are different? Share your impressions on the quality of the content as well. If you have any areas of uncertainty or disagreement, ask your professor.

ANALYSIS OF REAL-WORLD SAMPLE 2
Read the essay below and complete the analysis that follows.

"According to the NCA, 80% of Americans drink coffee, and more than half of the population drinks it every day."(Forbes) There are innumerable coffee shops scattered throughout various parts of the world. Consumers have thousands of options on where they choose to buy their caffeinated beverages. Many of us are unable to get our day started without a fresh cup of coffee. Luckily, we can always count on Starbucks to provide us with the best quality coffee available. Starbucks coffee has been a consumer favorite for many years. With there being countless of different coffee shops, many are left wondering why consumers remain loyal to Starbucks. The three main reasons why consumers choose Starbucks over other coffee shops and brands are the results of their availability, customer service, and the social media.

One of the reasons that consumers find themselves attached to Starbucks is its availability. Starbucks is constantly expanding and making itself more accessible to consumers. According to Starbucks.com, there are approximately 17,009 Starbucks coffee shops throughout the world. Consumers are drawn to Starbucks because they are conveniently located around cities and towns. Some may say that Starbucks shops are everywhere and have even become unavoidable. According to an article titled, "A Starbucks on Every Corner," Starbucks shops are vigorously growing. The article states, "Starbucks also is flooding some smaller cities. In Spokane, Wash., two Starbucks sit across from each other in a strip mall and a grocery store, close enough that baristas could toss pounds of coffee beans at one another if they wanted to." Starbucks acknowledges that consumers are not keen to waiting in long lines for their overpriced drinks. As expressed by the article, "A Starbucks on Every Corner," Starbucks solution to keep customers from waiting in long lines is to open a store near another store. I   n addition, most Starbucks stores are now offering drive through services that make it suitable for their busy, on the go customers to acquire their coffee without leaving their vehicle. Starbucks' drive through services offer costumers a full menu without the hassle of having to park their cars and stand in a line. Why drive to another coffee shop when there is a Starbucks conveniently located almost in every street corner? Consumers remain loyal to Starbucks because Starbucks is determined to remain accessible in every way possible.

Besides being conveniently available to consumers, Starbucks makes it a priority to provide its customers with a pleasant and comfortable environment. High quality customer service is another explanation to why Starbucks has a large scale of loyal customers. Starbucks is committed to not only giving its customers premium beverages, but also providing them with an enjoyable experience that keeps them coming back. In an article by Barbara Farfan, called "Starbucks Service Commitment, Starbucks Service Moment", she states that, "Back in February, Starbucks management made a bold move when they closed all of their 7,100 stores for 3 hours so that they could re-train their baristas on creating the best customer experience." Starbucks makes it a priority to hire individuals that will provide its customers with a joyful experience. In the book *Starbucks Experience: 5 principles for turning ordinary into extraordinary* by Joseph A. Michelli, he explains, " We each get to be part of a group that gets to make a huge difference in people's lives in a million small ways-just little moments like smiling as we hand you a drink, hand-crafting your beverage just the way you like it, and providing a comfy chair and a place to get away from it all without going very far." Starbucks recognizes that a friendly staff and a smile go a long way. Not only are customers greeted with a smile but people have the comfort in knowing that they can have their beverage remade if for some reason it does not meet their expectations. Starbucks dedication to provide superior customer service is one of the reasons why they continue to have faithful customers.

In addition to being accessible and having impressive customer service, Starbucks' consumer loyalty has a lot to do with the social media. Starbucks is utilizing the social media as a means to engage its customers and acquire new ones. According to thenextweb.com, "Starbucks has over 705,000 followers on twitter and over 5,428,000 fans on Facebook." Starbucks is giving its customers the opportunity to make suggestions and offer feedback on their products and services. Starbucks has become a consumer haven. It is not only a place to buy coffee but a place where students can study, business meetings can be held, and a place to simply relax. Starbucks is a trendy meeting place for people of all ages. It has even created their own language. People feel special when they know how to order off of the menu. Only at Starbucks will you hear somebody order a "venti, non-fat, upside down caramel macchiato." Customers feel like they belong to an elite group and those who ask for a "small" instead of a "tall" are quickly corrected. In an article by Lincoln Armstrong named "A Beginners Guide to Starbucks Drinks," he states, "The grammar of the Starbucks order determines the correct order of choices, while the vocabulary might include completely new words like "half-caf, misto or chai." There is even a dialect which can be a source of controversy, as in the differing opinions on the correct pronunciation of "venti." Is it "ven-TEE" or "ven-TAY?" If customers are unsure how to order a specific drink they can always access the Starbucks website or Facebook page. Starbucks knows how to make their customers feel important and like they are a member of a special and unique group. All consumers have to do to join is click the "like" button on Facebook or visit their nearest Starbucks store.

There are three main factors that contribute to Starbucks customer loyalty: availability, customer service, and the social media. Consumers do not have to travel far whenever they crave one of Starbucks tasty treats. They can expect to be greeted by a courteous staff and know that their order will be made precisely. Starbucks also uses the social media as a means to communicate with their customers and obtain new ones. Starbucks mission is "to inspire and nurture the human spirit-one person, one cup and one neighborhood at a time."

Works Cited

Armstrong, Lincoln. "A Beginners Guide to Starbucks Drinks." *HubPages*. Web. 14 Apr. 2011.

Bruce Horovitz. "Starbucks' growth strategy thinks outside the cup. " *Gannett News Service* 23 March 2011 ProQuest Newsstand, ProQuest. Web. 31 Mar. 2011.

"Coffee Perks - Forbes.com." *Information for the World's Business Leaders - Forbes.com.* Web. 31 Mar. 2011.

Gillespie, Elizabeth M. "New Drive-through Starbucks Grounds for Driving up Profits | The San Diego Union-Tribune." *San Diego News, Local, California and National News - SignOnSanDiego.com*. Web. 31 Mar. 2011.

Hanft | Apr, By Adam. "What You Can Learn from Starbucks, Customer Service Article - Inc. Article." *Small Business and Small Business Information for the Entrepreneur*. 01 Apr. 2005. Web. 31 Mar. 2011.

ANALYSIS

Now that you have read the sample essay, read it again and identify the following parts.

❖ Thesis Statement

❖ The three CAUSES

❖ Body Paragraph One Topic Sentence

❖ Support used

❖ References and style of reference (direct quotation, paraphrase)

❖ Body Paragraph Two Topic Sentence

❖ Support used

❖ Support used

❖ References and style of reference (direct quotation, paraphrase)

❖ Body Paragraph Three Topic Sentence

❖ Support used

❖ Support used

❖ References and style of reference (direct quotation, paraphrase)

❖ Conclusion

GROUP EXERCISE

Share your analysis with a partner or group. What observations do you have that are similar and what do you have that are different? Share your impressions on the quality of the content as well. If you have any areas of uncertainty or disagreement, ask your professor.

MODULE THREE - CAUSE OR EFFECT ESSAY WRITING ASSIGNMENT

Write a 5-paragraph essay on one of the following Groundhog Day topics.

Choice One
Eros, agape, and philia are three kinds of love. What are <u>the effects</u> of Phil being trapped in Groundhog Day on his attitude toward and the practice of these three kinds of love?

Choice Two
What effects does Phil's entrapment in Groundhog Day have on his inner, personal and professional worlds?

Choice Three
By the end of Groundhog Day, Phil has undeniably undergone a transformation and achieved a state of happiness he had not known before. Beyond the obvious entrapment in time, what are the primary causes of Phil's ultimate transformation?

Choice Four
Groundhog Day has been adopted by several faiths as an example of some of the principles of those faiths. Choose a religion and explain why Groundhog Day and its protagonists are valuable instruments in the teaching of that religion.

Essay Rules

1. Essay must be 1500-1750 words, typed, double spaced.
2. No first person singular.

3. No plagiarism.
4. Begin introduction with a quotation, statistic, or anecdote.
5. Thesis must be last sentence of introduction.
6. Each body paragraph must have at least two sources. Only one source can be a direct quotation. The other in-text source can be paraphrase, summary, indirect quotation.

DUE DATE: _____

ALTERNATE POSSIBLE CAUSE ESSAY TOPICS

1. Write an essay analyzing the primary causes of California's current economic crisis.

2. Write an essay analyzing the most significant causes of a historical event. (Do not revamp a History paper!)

3. Write an essay identifying a current environmental problem and analyze the three greatest causes of that problem.

ALTERNATE POSSIBLE EFFECT ESSAY TOPICS

1. Write an essay analyzing the primary effects of credit card companies recent behavior on the individual consumer.

2. Write an essay analyzing the most serious negative effects of homelessness on society.

3. Write an essay analyzing the effects of online universities on the higher education system.

CAUSE AND EFFECT PITFALLS (ROOKIE MISTAKES)

Now that you know how to research your topic and you have mastered the structure of the thesis and topic sentences, some students go into the cause and effect essay with the idea that they do not need proof. It is part of the reason that we've done so much research in this chapter. Many students mistake their opinions for solid support. Just because you think it is obvious that healthcare needs to move in a certain direction – that doesn't count as support. You make the observation and then you carefully research and find others that agree with your opinion. That's when the cause and effect papers are most, well for want of a better word, effective.

WRITING BREAK 5

GRAMMAR

One of the most common grammar mistakes from writers is related to sentence boundaries. When writing, you may use a comma to separate two sentences, or you may be so involved in your content that you string sentences together. Both of these cases lead to mistakes called comma splices and run-on (fused) sentences. Another mistake is where you leave a sentence unfinished and that is a fragment. Very simple illustrations of each of the mistakes are below.

COMMA SPLICE

Michael loved writing essays with all his heart, he just couldn't put the pen down once he had an idea.

RUN-ON SENTENCE

Michael loved writing essays with all his heart he just couldn't put the pen down once he had an idea.

It is important to notice that this is really the same mistake – a lack of recognition as to where the sentence should end and how you can punctuate that or connect the ideas. Notice also that inserting a comma or removing a comma does not fix anything –it just creates a different mistake!

How can you correct these?

SOLUTION ONE - ADD A PERIOD

Michael loved writing essays with all his heart. He just couldn't put the pen down once he had an idea.

SOLUTION TWO - ADD A SEMI-COLON

Michael loved writing essays with all his heart; he just couldn't put the pen down once he had an idea.

SOLUTION THREE - CONNECT THE IDEAS AND PUNCTUATE APPROPRIATELY

Michael loved writing essays with all his heart, and he just couldn't put the pen down once he had an idea.

Because Michael loved writing essays with all his heart, he just couldn't put the pen down once he had an idea.

Michael loved writing essays with all his heart. Therefore, he just couldn't put the pen down once he had an idea.

Michael loved writing essays with all his heart. Therefore, it is no surprise that he just couldn't put the pen down once he had an idea.

FRAGMENT

Because Michelle loved English class.

A fragment is an incomplete sentence. Notice how the sentence above has a subject (Michelle) and a verb (loved) but is still incomplete. The "because" is a subordinating conjunction and this whole clause needs to be attached to another clause in order for the sentence to be whole.

SOLUTION - add another clause!
Because Michelle loved English class, she worked very hard every day.

Microsoft word recognizes typically recognizes fragments, run-ons, and comma splices with its squiggly green underlining, so take advantage of that option as you write your essays. Also, use that option to help you learn from your mistakes.

WRITING MODULE FOUR

COMPARISON/CONTRAST ESSAYS

To be more precise this chapter will focus on either comparison OR contrast essay.

Comparison shows the <u>similarities</u> between two objects or objectives.

Contrast shows <u>differences</u> between two objects or objectives.

Why can't I compare differences? The same reason you can't contrast similarities. In reality at a certain level, yes, you can do both but not yet. Wait until you're a doctoral student studying the differences in similar literary critique methodology. For now, just keep the ideas in your head that if you set out to compare, you're looking for three similarities, and contrast is about three differences. If you don't know why I keep saying three, remember, it's a five-paragraph essay world out there.

We are going to jump right into an exercise that should help you understand the value of this mode of rhetoric. Again, we start out simple but it will become more difficult as the chapter continues.

IN-CLASS EXERCISE

BEFORE-CLASS PREPARATION
Each student should write 300 words about a memorable vacation and bring it to class.

IN-CLASS
Get together in small groups. Choose one person who had a very similar or very different vacations. Decide whether you would like to compare or contrast your own summer break to your partner's. (ONE PARTNER)

Formulate an explicit topic sentence that shows three areas of similarity or difference. DO NOT DO BOTH. Then write a paragraph comparing or contrasting your break. Now, you know by not that this book does not support the use of first person singular in your academic essay; therefore, how are you going to do this exercise? Well, it is actually easy to avoid.

Personal Topic Sentence - needs to be changed

John and I had a very different experience on their vacations from the point of view of travel, free-time and romance.

Non-personal Topic Sentence

John and Maria had a very different experience on their vacations from the point of view of travel, free-time and romance.

> "I try to contrast; life today is full of contrast...
> We have to change."
> **Gianni Versace**

PARAGRAPH STRUCTURE OUTLINE

It is easy to forget what a paragraph looks like, so below is an outline for a contrast paragraph and for a comparison paragraph. This should help you stay focused in both structure and content.

ASSIGNMENT

Write the paragraph and bring the completed version to class. You need it to do the next exercise.

Contrast Paragraph Outline (Point by Point)

Explicit Topic Sentence: _____

_____

Transition + SP 1 (Difference 1): _____

_____

    Details:

Transition + SP 2 (Difference 2): _____

_____

    Details:

Transition + SP 3 (Difference 3): _____

_____

    Details:

Concluding Sentence: _____

_____

Comparison Paragraph Outline (Point by Point)

Explicit Topic Sentence: _____

_____

Transition + SP 1 (Similarity 1): _____

_____

    Details:

Transition + SP 2 (Similarity 2): _____

_____

    Details:

Transition + SP 3 (Similarity 3): _____

_____

    Details:

Concluding Sentence: _____

_____

Terminology

Below are some transitions that can be helpful in comparison and contrast.
Put the following words into the appropriate column. Can you think of other phrases?

In contrast	likewise	unlike
Again	still	but
Regardless	in the same way	also
Despite	while	like
Compared to	nevertheless	as well as
Different from	similarly	in contrast to
By the same token	even though	however
But	just as...so too...	although
Conversely	similar to	yet
On the one hand...on the other hand		

Comparison	Contrast

APPLICATION - Analyze your own work

Bring out the Summer Break Paragraphs you wrote. Read through them and circle any comparison/contrast transitions that you used. How many do you have? Too many? Too few?

REVISE YOUR WORK

Rewrite your paragraph and add at least three of the comparison/contrast transitions to the body. If you already had three or more, look at the boxes on the previous page and see if you can change some of them to phrases you didn't use or don't use very often.

Do you notice how the addition of these transitions helps your paragraph?

PEER REVIEW

After adding the transitions, find a partner and exchange papers. Be sure to exchange both copies. Can you tell the difference? After reading each other's work, talk with your partner to note the differences that you found.

Comparison and Contrast Essay

Now that we have an idea of how to compare and contrast narrative writings (your experience in summer break is an example) we need to broaden out to the more general use of comparison and contrast in an academic definition.
How do we use comparison to inform a reader about a subject? How do we use contrast to put a topic in a better light? Can these two methods of "thought exploration" take us anywhere? I'm sure that you have guessed since there is an entire chapter on this subject that the answer is yes.

The first part of any assignment is choosing what to compare or contrast. The best way to determine which you should do with a given subject is to ask yourself which would be easier? Is it easier to compare or contrast Madonna to Brittany Spears? Is it easier to compare or contrast the New York Times and the Los Angeles Times? Finally, is it easier to compare or contrast Joyce to Dostoyevsky?

Once you have determined which is easier, you then should eliminate it as a potential paper topic. Do you want to know three similarities between Coke and Pepsi? The two are so similar that your audience will be reaching for a Mountain Dew by page three and Mountain Dew may be the least appealing soft drink ever mass marketed (my apologies to the "extreme" crowd out there who love it). Now the contrast might be a little more interesting:

Soft drink	Contrast 1 Sweetness	Contrast 2 Carbonation	Contrast 3 Ingredients
Pepsi	High	Low	Phosphoric acid
Coke	Low	High	Citric Acid
Mountain Dew	Off the charts hit the wall running sweet	I can't tell, my head is still spinning	Hydrochloric acid

Table 6.1 As you might be able to tell, I did take some liberties with the Mountain Dew example.

EMAIL OR WEB SPECIAL

Go to youtube.com (or any other free Internet resource) and find two movies that are set in classrooms. Write down the links below:

As you watch and decide consider the following: Who? What? When? Where? (not just a classroom, but urban classroom, rural classroom, foreign classroom) Why?

	Link One	Link Two
Who:		
What		
When		
Where		
Why		

Do you want to compare or contrast these two clips? Why?

Bring your completed table and clips to class. Now the instructor will choose one or two students to play their examples for the class. Did they choose comparison or contrast? Can you make a case that they should have chosen the other? For example, a classroom set in 2050, might be a cool comparison against a classroom set in 1920. All of the differences are apparent, but how do the students still have the same role, and how does the teacher interact with them? Times change, technology changes, but stunningly the teacher-student interaction probably does not seem so different. Isn't that a bit interesting?

One might contrast two urban classrooms by showing that even though they are both dingy and remedial, one class still is engaged with the instructor and capable of learning and the other is not. How did you determine this from the clip? Isn't that an interesting way to look at two situations that might at first glance appear to be totally the same?

Comparison and contrast when done correctly turns a topic into an exploration of new ways to look into a central issue by exploring similarities or differences. Search for the best way to achieve that goal by throwing out the easy route. It will help you prepare a paper that does not merely exist for the sake of an assignment, but one that engages a reader and makes them think of a topic in a different (or similar) light. Interesting other people also has the intriguing side-effect of interesting the writer in the process. It is hard to be bored while fascinating someone else.

ELEMENTS OF THE COMPARISON/CONTRAST ESSAY

The Comparison or Contrast Thesis

As you now know because this book keeps telling you, every essay needs a thesis statement, and a cause essay needs a cause thesis. That means that the thesis should not only indicate the topic but also the mode (comparison or contrast) of the essay. In this way, the writer is very clear on the purpose of the essay. In this mode of rhetoric we want an explicit thesis that defines three differences or similarities. Why three? Well, the five paragraph essay comes standard with three body paragraphs. The three body paragraphs should each illustrate one clear and unified difference or similarity and so three parts in the thesis lead directly into this model. (Remember the Writing Break earlier where this was explained?)

Example Thesis Statements

Read the sample thesis statements below and identify the topic, the three differences or similarities, and any words or phrases that indicate the mode (comparison or contrast). Decide if each thesis is effective.

THESIS ONE
There are three essential similarities between Gandhi's leadership style and Clinton's leadership style.

THESIS TWO
Although Brittney Spears and Christina Aguilera shared an early bond and career, their musical styles, their life choices, and their vocal abilities put the two performers into very different classes.

THESIS THREE
Despite their lifelong competition, Bill Gates and Steve Jobs show surprising similarities in business acumen, personal values, and professional ethics.

TOPIC SENTENCES AND SUPPORT IN A COMPARISON/CONTRAST ESSAY.

You should also remember that every paragraph begins with a topic sentence. Coherence between paragraphs is an important part of essays. The topic sentences of your body paragraphs are tied directly to your thesis statement and the essay mode. Just as you include the overall essay topic, the sub-topic, and the mode in the thesis, so too do you include these things in the topic sentence. Look at the sample thesis from earlier:

Thesis: *Although Brittney Spears and Christina Aguilera shared an early bond and career, their musical styles, their life choices, and their vocal abilities put the two performers into very different classes.*

Using the thesis above, it should be easy to construct topic sentences for each body paragraph.

EXAMPLE ONE
Topic Sentence Body Paragraph One:
One difference between Spears and Aguilera is in their musical styles.
Topic Sentence Body Paragraph Two:
Another difference between the singers Spears and Aguilera is in their life choices.

Topic Sentence Body Paragraph Three:
The final difference between Spears and Aguilera is in their vocal abilities.

These topic sentences are fine and they do the work of a topic sentence. They have the key components and quite frankly, that makes them work. The question that you as a writer must ask is, can you do better? Look at the following two examples of transitions and topic sentences and discuss what makes them different from the first and from each other. Which do you prefer?

EXAMPLE TWO

Thesis: *Although Brittney Spears and Christina Aguilera shared an early bond and career, their musical styles, their life choices, and their vocal abilities put the two performers into very different classes.*

Topic Sentence Body Paragraph One:
       One important difference between Spears and Aguilera is in their musical styles.

Topic Sentence Body Paragraph Two:
       Another key difference between the singers Spears and Aguilera is in their life choices.

Topic Sentence Body Paragraph Three:
       The most telling difference between Spears and Aguilera is in their vocal abilities.

EXAMPLE THREE

Thesis: *Although Brittney Spears and Christina Aguilera shared an early bond and career, their musical styles, their life choices, and their vocal abilities put the two performers into very different classes.*

Topic Sentence Body Paragraph One:
       One interesting difference between Spears and Aguilera is in their musical styles.

Topic Sentence Body Paragraph Two:
       In addition to distinct musical styles, Spears and Aguilera have made choices that set their personal lives apart.

Topic Sentence Body Paragraph Three:
       While musical styles and personal lives show clear differences between the two singers, the ultimate separation of Spears and Aguilera is in their vocal abilities.

TOPIC SENTENCE EXERCISE

Using the given thesis from earlier, write transitions and topic sentences for each of the three body paragraphs. Remember, the sub-points are there, so this really is an exercises on connecting the opening of a paragraph with the rest of your essay.

THESIS: *Despite their lifelong competition, Bill Gates and Steve Jobs show surprising similarities in business acumen, personal values, and professional ethics.*

Topic Sentence Body Paragraph One:

_____

_____

Topic Sentence Body Paragraph Two:

_____

_____

Topic Sentence Body Paragraph Three:

_____

_____

TOPIC SENTENCE EXERCISE 2

Using the given thesis, write transitions and topic sentences for each of the three body paragraphs. Remember, the sub-points are there, so this really is an exercises on connecting the opening of a paragraph with the rest of your essay.

THESIS: Even though Coca Cola and Pepsi are two successful companies in the world of business, there are remarkable differences in their product, in their marketing approaches, and in their distribution channels.

Topic Sentence Body Paragraph One:

_____

_____

Topic Sentence Body Paragraph Two:

_____

_____

Topic Sentence Body Paragraph Three:

_____

_____

Quality Check
Did you step up your coherence and topic sentences between the first exercise and the second? If you did not, go back and do so; otherwise, how do you expect to improve your writing?

Comparison and Contrast Essay Structure

You need to read about structure because there are two different ways to put together this essay.

WRITING STYLE 1 - POINT-BY-POINT

We will start and put an emphasis on point-by-point structure. This is because it tends to lead to stronger organization among students who are first experiencing the mode of rhetoric. You'll understand better after both have been introduced.

Let's say that we are comparing **two authors A and B**

The point-by-point structure of that paper might look something like this:

Thesis Statement: Author A and Author B are both interesting writers who display commonalities in style, characters, and settings.

Body Paragraph 1
Topic Sentence: One area of similarity between A and B is in their literary styles.

❖ Point 1: Both authors are descriptive. Introduce examples of the descriptions of both authors then proceed to analyze the similarities

❖ Point 2: Both authors use first person narrative for tension. Introduce examples of the descriptions of both authors then proceed to analyze the similarities

❖ Point 3: Both authors explore characterization by psychological analysis. Introduce examples of the descriptions of both authors then proceed to analyze the similarities

Body paragraph 2
Topic Sentence: In addition to literary stlye, A and B pen similar characters in their works.

❖ Point 1: Both authors write about lower-class heroes. Introduce examples of the descriptions of both authors then proceed to analyze the similarities

❖ Point 2: Both authors have strong female characters that betray the hero. Introduce examples of the descriptions of both authors then proceed to analyze the similarities

❖ Point 3: Both authors make the rich and powerful people the antagonists. Introduce examples of the descriptions of both authors then proceed to analyze the similarities

Body Paragraph 3
Topic Sentence: The final commonality between A and B is in the settings of their literary creations.

❖ Point 1: Both authors set their stories in cities under siege. Introduce examples of the descriptions of both authors then proceed to analyze the similarities

❖ Point 2: Both authors have their heroes living in poverty. Introduce examples of the descriptions of both authors then proceed to analyze the similarities

❖ Point 3: Both authors have their heroes journey to better places in the book. Introduce examples of the descriptions of both authors then proceed to analyze the similarities

Notice how each paragraph addresses both authors one after the other. Each point about one work is immediately compared to the similar point in the other work. It makes for a very balanced analysis of the two authors. None of the points get misplaced because if an idea is brought up about one author it is immediately addressed in the other author. This organization helps many writers keep a strong structure of what is being compared.

ACTIVITY
STEP ONE - Out-of-class preparation

Contrast two articles
Go to findarticles.com or refdesk.com and find an article that presents a critical description of a world leader(it can be about a certain policy or his general leadership).

Now go to a website that promotes the leader. It can be a homepage or campaign page or an advocacy page.

STEP TWO

Write a point-by-point paragraph talking about the differences in how the leader is presented in these two forums. Once you've completed the paragraph imagine that you just looked at the advocacy page and you'll understand why instructors do not always trust the Internet. Bring your paragraphs to class.

A blank paragraph outline is below to help you stay structured. It does not replace a full paragraph; it is there simply as a reminder of structure.

Explicit Topic Sentence: _____

_____

Transition + SP 1 (Difference 1): _____

_____

    Details:

Transition + SP 2 (Difference 2): _____

_____

    Details:

Transition + SP 3 (Difference 3): _____

_____

    Details:

Concluding Sentence: _____

STEP THREE - PEER REVIEW

Conduct a peer review of the paragraphs. Exchange books and answer the following questions about the paragraph that you are reading.
Is the topic sentence explicit and clear?
Does it name the two subjects?
Does it have at least three supporting points?
Do those supporting points have clear transitions?
Is the paragraph coherent?
Is the paragraph on topic?
Circle all the words/phrases that indicate that the paragraph is a contrast.

WRITING STYLE 2 - BLOCK METHOD

There is another effective method of comparison and contrast, but any student who tries it should be careful to proofread and make certain that every point is addressed in terms of comparison or contrast.

Block Method

Let's take our authors comparison and flip it into a contrast.

Thesis Statement: Author 1 and Author 2 may seem similar but close analysis reveals distinct differences in their literary styles, characters, and settings.

Body paragraph 1

Author 1

*   ❖ Style

        Details on Author 1 that support the style analysis

*   ❖ Characters

        Details Author 1 that support the character analysis

*   ❖ Setting

        Details Author 1 that support the setting analysis

Body paragraph 2 – VERY STRONG TRANSITION SENTENCE BRINGING THE TWO TOGETHER

143

Author 2

- ❖ Differences in style (with references back to Author 1)
  - Details that support the style analysis
- ❖ Differences in characters (with references back to Author 1)
  - Details that support the character analysis
- ❖ Differences in setting (with references back to Author 1)
  - Details that support the setting analysis

The problem with block method (and it is more of a problem with the execution than the actual method) is that some students treat it like a report on each subject and then never connect the specific similarities or differences between the two authors. If I tell you all about one author and then tell you all about another, is that really a contrast? It might be two different stories, but without analysis that highlights the importance of each difference, it's just a mishmash of facts that are searching for something to pull them together. Don't expect the reader to pull together what is interesting from your comparison or contrast. Tell them why you are doing this exercise, and why the ideas you've chosen to compare or contrast are so interesting when viewed in this way.

SAMPLE BLOCK STYLE

Below is a sample of a very simple block method. Notice that there are no sources or research in here – its purpose is solely to show off the block method.

John and Jane are both successful students and are at the top of their class. This is all the more surprising when one considers their extremely different, almost diametrically opposed, approaches to studying.

John is a bookworm. Whenever you cannot find him, just go to the library and he will be there with his nose in a book. He doesn't really mind what he reads as long as he has a book in his hand, he is happy. He transfers this love of reading into his studying, devouring as much information as he possibly can through the written word. In addition to this passion for books is John's love of writing. He is at his most content when he has papers to write for school. He loves to sit at his computer, research the topic, and then put his ideas down. Best of all, he loves being able to move text around and trying to express himself in many different ways and then going back and deciding which he likes best. When it comes to tests and exams, John is in his element. He goes over his meticulous notes, rewriting and adding information where necessary. After this, he visits the professor to check that his information is accurate. Then he begins his timetable of self-testing. He wakes up an hour earlier than usual in order to quiz himself on the subject matter being tested. If the exam involves writing an essay, he will practice writing different essays for the potential essay topics. His friends describe him as obsessive, but he doesn't mind because he knows he performs best when he is well prepared.

Unlike John, Jane does not actually pick up a book for pleasure. She doesn't dislike reading, but she does need a purpose. For that reason, you will only find her in a library when she knows exactly what she wants. You certainly won't see her in there just for the pleasure of being surrounded by books. When it comes to collecting information, Jane would much rather watch a documentary on the subject than sit down and read about it. Another difference between John and Jane is that Jane does not enjoy the writing process. That does not mean she is not an excellent writer; in fact she is very talented. However, the thought of sitting at a computer and having to type paragraphs and organize ideas does not strongly appeal to her. She certainly doesn't share John's pleasure of editing and re-editing. When she has papers due, she waits until the last possible minute, sits down and the computer and starts typing. While this may seem to imply that Jane has not been thoughtfully preparing her essay, this would be an unfair assumption. Jane has been mulling the topic over in the back of her mind since the paper was assigned. Somewhat subconsciously, Jane has been writing the essay in her head, so when she does actually sit down at the computer, she is more than ready to write her paper. The third and perhaps most pronounced difference between John and Jane's approach to studying can be seen in test preparation. While John is the master of preparation, Jane is the queen of memory and intuition. Like John, she takes excellent notes. However, she also has an outstanding aural memory. This means that when she reads her notes, she can actually remember what the professor said, and on occasion, she can even hear the professor's voice rather like a tape recorder. Therefore, when taking exams, she simply uses her memory and often can be seen talking to herself during the actual exam. Obviously, she is not really talking to herself but vocalizing what she is hearing in her head.

ACTIVITY

Read the block sample above again. This time identify all the comparison or contrast markers that you can find. Within each Supporting Point, mark how many references back to John there are in the Jane paragraph.

Share your analysis with a peer and then with the class. What can you take from this exercise and apply to your own writing?

PRACTICE

If you are planning on writing a block-style essay, you should practice this method, so take the paragraph you wrote earlier in point-by-point (remember the one contrasting leaders) and switch it to a block paragraph or two block paragraphs. This will give you a more realistic idea of what writing in this style is actually like. Also, if you just want to practice writing, you could try this exercise. Ask your professor for his/her direction.

REAL-WORLD EXAMPLE FOR ANALYSIS

Read the essay below and the complete the analysis questions that follow.

"In the future, everyone will be world-famous for 15 minutes" (Andy Warhol, 1968). These famous words are now eerily becoming a reality. With the expanding technology of communication, people are finding new ways to reach out to the public and some are, literally, becoming famous overnight. These new types of celebrities aren't the young breakout stars of Hollywood blockbusters, nor are they the fresh captivating faces of independent films. These are the celebrities who became famous through reality TV shows and the internet. These are two different methods used by people, who would normally have gone through life as an anonymous face, to get their shot at fame. Reality show fame and internet fame are much alike because of three primary similarities: they are both all about self-promotion, they provide a chance to gain media attention, and fame from both either method is sure to quickly fade.

　　The first similarity between internet fame and reality show fame is that rigorous self-promotion is the key to obtain and sustain the fame that come from both methods. For any struggling actor or musician looking to get recognition for their work, self-promotion is a major first step to get taken seriously. For someone looking for fame by appearing on a reality show or by way of the internet, it's all about the promoting of oneself as a real person who audiences will want to watch. It is also the only element working to make fame possible, as it is very difficult getting taken seriously by people in the entertainment business if one is known as the kid messing around with lightsabers in an internet video or as the winner of last season's "Big Brother". Then again, people who cast reality shows want someone who is real and will let their personality shine through.

As pointed out on a website for Latin American Media and Marketing, the idea of a reality show "takes ordinary people, sets them up in extraordinary situations on a world stage with other similarly commonplace individuals, and makes them the focus of a nation's attention". The concept of a reality show is not to follow actors, but people who are "satisfactorily every-day individuals for fans to willfully suspend their disbelief" (Soong, Roland). This means that people casting reality shows want someone who can be themselves in an interesting way so that the audience will get hooked on the show. This requires a smart and strategic approach in self-promoting by reality show celebrities because "reality TV participants come from all walks of life. Whether you're gay or straight...Christian or Buddhist, Black or white, it is easy to turn on reality TV and spot someone like yourself whisked away into an adventurous or luxurious lifestyle. We experience a vicarious thrill seeing ordinary people like us compete for fabulous prizes" (Nutt, Amy). Much like landing on a reality show, the internet provides a great source for unknown, ordinary people to get discovered. Julia Allison, a bona fide celebrity from the internet, has gained fame, simply from having her own blogging website. Writer Jason Tanz provides some insight on how she made it possible: "Julia Allison can't act. She can't sing. She's not rich. But thanks to a genius for self-promotion, she's become an Internet celebrity". Tanz also goes on to point out that for her, self-promotion means posting her most flattering pictures on her MySpace page. "Traditionally, it takes an army of publicists, a well-connected family, or a big-budget ad campaign to make this kind of splash. But Allison has done it on her own and on the cheap, armed only with an insatiable need for attention and a healthy helping of Web savvy" (Wired Magazine, 15 July 2008). She's only using what the internet has given her, and in order to be a good publicist, self-promotion is a crucial step one must take to gain the fame and attention they are seeking.

Another similarity between fame from reality TV shows and fame from the internet is the opportunity that is given to gain media attention and work among other celebrities. With so many different types of reality shows on television, there's bound to be a cast member somewhere among them that is liked by a majority of its viewers. These people can be seen by the entertainment industry as a great hook for future reality shows and competitions on television. A writer for a reality TV show website notices that "many of

147

the 'stars' of those shows are parlaying their fifteen minutes of fame into a television career, whether we like it or not. Many VH1 countdown shows include comments from reality TV show stars such as Ralphie May (Last Comedian Standing) and Evan Marriott (Joe Millionaire) among others" ("Why is Reality TV So Big?"). The night of a reality TV show premier is similar to the minutes that follow a newly posted internet video. Through word of mouth and forwarding emails, a seemingly harmless video can easily get spread through cyberspace like wildfire, and whoever is in the video, can easily become an instant celebrity. A specific case of this happened when 19 year-old, amateur videographer, Gary Brolsma, posted a clip of himself dancing along to a Romanian pop song on the internet. "...the website newgrounds.com, a clearinghouse for online videos and animation, placed a link to Mr. Brolsma on its home page and, soon, there was a river of attention: 'Good Morning America' came calling and he appeared. CNN and VH1 broadcast the clip" (Feuer, Alan; George, Jason). Writer, David Thair provides a theory that suggests that media attention is the goal many internet celebrity hopefuls have in mind: "it seems that "web celebrities" are going to be ever more frequently making the transition from the internet to broadcast media...And a surprising crew of the internet's fringe celebrities is hoping they've gained enough combined popular recognition to actually have some influence over public affairs" (Thair, David). It's becoming more common to turn on the TV and see a new internet sensation replacing a movie star in the hot seat.

Lastly, the fame that comes from the internet or being on a reality TV show is commonly short-lived. For many reality show cast members, the combination of annoying too many viewers and bad publicity can be the reason for a short-lived career in the entertainment industry. Since reality TV show alumni consist of ordinary people instead of trained actors, they often aren't prepared for the demanding and sometimes cruel world that comes along with being famous. "While there are certainly many more reality stars who may have questionable lifestyles, you really have to wonder what effect the shows have had on them, or if it's simply the fact that they were already at risk for odd behavior and are now just under the public microscope a little more" (Anderson, Angela). While acting out simply for the publicity can be a career ending mistake, so can being on a reality show in the first place. Dean O'Loughin, who appeared on the second season of the show 'Big Brother' was a struggling musician and found the fame from the show difficult to deal with, stating in an interview, "I didn't really think the TV show would launch my music career into the stratosphere but it surprised me to find it did the complete opposite. Suddenly, I was seen as a bit of a joke, as a reality TV star trying to have a musical career....'Big Brother' killed it stone dead" (The London Independent, 7 Feb. 2004). Much like the quickly fading star of a reality TV show cast member, an internet celebrity can easily overstay their welcome in the Hollywood limelight through overexposure. The irate Britney Spears fan, whose video of himself poring his heart out, literally, became famous within 24 hours of posting it. His video made its rounds through emails and is now embracing his fame with more videos of ridiculous behavior. One comedy writer begs society to be more cautious in the future, "as we all must share in this most unpleasant aspect of Internet stardom...and think twice the next time" (Glagg, Alex, Best Week Ever). In addition, the knowledge of how the entertainment business truly works contributes to bad choices and missed opportunities. The Britney Spears fan is used as an example when he "apparently passed up the 'Kimmel' and 'Today' phases" and, instead went straight to daytime talk show 'Maury', noted as a "nail in the coffin" for anyone's career (Hopper, Dan, Best Week Ever). With little guidance, an internet celebrity will be able to hold the attention of the public for only so long. In both cases, fame is often misunderstood and poorly executed by these overnight sensations.

In a world where "at almost any given moment during the day, you can turn on your television and find a reality TV show on" ("Why is Reality TV So Big?"), there's a new breed of celebrities to represent ordinary, everyday people. When tabloid magazines are no longer only reserved for Hollywood celebrities, but also for a crazed fan of a pop singer letting his emotions get the best of him in an internet video, one must ask: Is Hollywood busting at the seams? These days, true talent takes a backseat when someone is looking for instant fame. Because of the easy accessibility of the internet and growing popularity of a reality show for every premise imaginable, instant fame isn't hard to come by. As long as no one minds that the type of fame they'll achieve is, most likely, the kind that fades as quickly as it came.

ANALYSIS

Now that you have read the sample essay, read it again and identify the following parts.

- ❖ Thesis Statement
- ❖ Body Paragraph One Topic Sentence
- ❖ Support used and references
- ❖ Body Paragraph Two Topic Sentence
- ❖ Support used and references
- ❖ Body Paragraph Three Topic Sentence
- ❖ Support used and references
- ❖ Conclusion
- ❖ Comparison/Contrast Markers and Transitions

IN-CLASS EXERCISE

Share your analysis with a partner or group. What observations do you have that are similar and what do you have that are different? Share your impressions on the quality of the content as well. If you have any areas of uncertainty or disagreement, ask your professor.

REAL-WORLD EXAMPLE 1 FOR ANALYSIS

Read the following essay and complete the analysis questions that follow it.

A Lot In Common

"...I don't know. I mean, perfect is a lot to expect from something, right? We all have our faults" (Dessen, 118). The truth of this poignant quote from Sarah Dessen's novel *Keeping the Moon* echoes through Steve Martin's *The Pleasure of My Company*, as both main characters struggle to find acceptance and contentment. Though the books were written for two separate audiences, they share many elements of character development, themes, and narration style.

In both *Keeping the Moon* and *The Pleasure of My Company* the main characters display tremendous personal growth as they interact with outside forces. Sarah Dessen's protagonist, fifteen-year-old Nicole "Colie" Sparks, struggles with her weight and an undeserved reputation as a slut. Steve Martin's narrator, thirty-one-year old Daniel Pecan Cambridge, daily battles his autism and obsessive-compulsive disorder. Both characters overcome the things that originally restrict and confine them within themselves. Colie spends her summer getting know Morgan, Isabel, and Norman, three very different people who all help her to see beyond her past and find who she really is. The girls give Colie a physical makeover, while all three help her complete an emotional, mental alteration. As Colie comes to believe in herself, she is finally able to put her past behind her and embrace the future. She explains, "The strange thing was that I *felt* different. As if something pulled taut for so long had eased back, everything that had strained settling into place: those forty-five pounds finally gone for good" (Dessen, 202). Similarly, Daniel also learns to move beyond the restrictions of his autism and OCD. With the help of Zandy Alice Allen, the sweet girl from the Rite Aid, Daniel overcomes his obsessions, the little "quirks" that formerly made daily life so difficult for him. As he says, "Months went by and she got to the heart of me. With a cheery delicacy she divided my obsessions into three categories: acceptable, unacceptable, and hilarious... We compromised on the lights, but eventually Zandy's humor...made the obsession too unnerving to indulge in" (Martin, 161). Both of these characters began with emotional baggage that was difficult for them to work around, but with love and encouragement, they put their circumstances behind them and began to believe in themselves. Colie lost her self-consciousness and Daniel lost his neurotic behaviors, both while learning to embrace life and its abnormalities. Kirkus Reviews commented that *Keeping the Moon* is, "Rich in sharply observed relationships...and characters who are not afraid to pick themselves up and try again..." Likewise, Patrick O'Kelley noted in his review of *The Pleasure of My Company* that, "...Martin insists through Daniel – a man haunted by horrors of his own making – that there is possibility for compassion, that broken lives can actually be healed." Both novels present characters that are blinded by obstructions of their own creation and have to reach within themselves to find healing and contentment.

 Keeping the Moon and *The Pleasure of My Company* also display similarities in their themes of love and judging. Both Colie and Daniel look for love in the wrong places and make the wrong judgments about other people. Colie first turns to a boy who is only interested in a sexual relationship, before finding Norman, who loves her for the person she is. Daniel fantasizes about the beautiful realtor Elizabeth and admires his student-therapist Clarissa before discovering that the Rite Aid pharmacist, Zandy, is interested in him in spite of his mental condition. For Colie, Norman goes from being "Hippie Norman. So *not* the guy for me" (Dessen, 96) to someone she imagines "leaning closer, tucking the hair behind my ear, again. I'd smile, then" (Dessen, 189). As Colie changes, mentally, physically, and emotionally, her idea of the perfect guy changes too. She learns to look past appearances and instead judge someone by their actions. Norman's long hair, slow gait, and artistic quirks no longer both Colie, because she appreciates his kind, generous, forgiving nature. Likewise, Daniel comes to see that Zandy is the right girl for him, though he had only ever admired her from a distance before. He sums it up simply in this: "Zandy Alice Allen proved to be the love of my life" (Martin, 161). Daniel had mistakenly thought that because Elizabeth was the most beautiful woman he had ever seen, she was therefore the best match for him. Then he thought that he shared a special bond with Clarissa, though she never saw Daniel in a romantic way. After searching for love in the wrong places and misjudging those who turned out to best compliment their personalities, both Colie and Daniel realize that love was right in front of them all along. The theme of mistaken first impressions was common between the two books. A research project from the Department of Psychology at the Loyola University of New Orleans concluded that although first impressions are often based on physical appearance, as two people get to know each other, personality becomes more important in the continuation of the relationship (Gonzales). Both Colie and Daniel display this in their interactions with other people and come to discover that first impressions aren't always correct.

Colie and Daniel also display a similar style in their narrations. Since both of them have experienced ostracization, they tend to view the world from a different perspective. Colie is uncomfortably familiar with being made fun of and having people talk about her behind her back. This contributes to her first, mistaken impressions Morgan, Isabel, and Norman. As she explains on first meeting the Morgan and Isabel, "I'd had enough experience with girls in groups to be on my guard" (Dessen, 24). Later she reveals more about this "experience:" "There's a kind of radar you get, after years of being talked about and made fun of by other people. You can almost smell when it's about to happen, can recognize instantly the sound of a hushed voice, lowered just enough to make whatever is said okay" (Dessen, 61). After being made fun of for so long, Colie reveals these observations about human nature. And it's true: people do lower their voices when they are about to spread a rumor or share a juicy piece of gossip. Her unique perspective adds another aspect to the story. In the same way, Daniel's mathematical prowess allows him to see the world in a different light. He finds it easiest to explain things in terms of numbers and geometry. During one of his "therapy" sessions with Clarissa, her phone rings and she glances at the caller ID before turning it off. But the ever-observant Daniel sees much more than most people would. "Then something exciting happened. Her cell phone rang. It was exciting because what crossed her face ranged wildly on the map of human emotion. And oh, did I divide that moment up into millionths…" (Martin, 31). In the submoments that Daniel creates from this occurrence, he is able to describe every emotion that must have been going through Clarissa's mind at the moment. When she thought she was analyzing Daniel, he was actually doing a much more thorough job of analyzing *her*. Both Colie and Daniel show a deeper understanding of human nature and this comes through in their narrations. They are able to dissect a wide range of emotions and explain them further. Their life experiences have made them more sensitive to *why* people act in the way they do.

Although Sarah Dessen and Steve Martin wrote for two completely different audiences, their books share many common elements of character development, themes, and narration style. Both *Keeping the Moon* and *The Pleasure of My Company* present insecure, uncertain characters who overcome their fears (with help from friends) and develop into strong, confident individuals. This transformation, so frequent in literature, may reflect a human desire to overcome our own challenges and embrace life for what it is.

Works Cited

Dessen, Sarah. *Keeping the Moon*. New York: Speak, 2004. Print.

Gonzales, Casey L. MS. Loyola University of New Orleans. *First Impressions: The Effect of Physical Attractiveness and Personality on Relationships*. Missouri Western State University, 2009. Web. 20 June 2010. <http://clearinghouse.missouriwestern.edu /manuscripts/197.php>.

Kirkus Associates, LP. Rev. of *Keeping the Moon*, by Sarah Dessen. *Amazon.com*. Amazon.com, Inc., 1999. Web. 20 June 2010. <http://www.amazon.com/gp/product/product-description/0142401765/ref=dp_proddesc_0?ie=UTF8&n=283155&s=books>.

Martin, Steve. *The Pleasure of My Company: a Novel*. New York: Hyperion, 2003. Print.

O'Kelley, Patrick. Rev. of *The Pleasure of My Company*, by Steve Martin. *Amazon.com*. Amazon.com, Inc., 2003. Web. 20 June 2010. <http://www.amazon.com/gp/product/ product-description/0786869216/ref=dp_proddesc_0?ie=UTF8&n=283155&s=books>.

ANALYSIS

Now that you have read the sample essay, read it again and identify the following parts.

❖ Thesis Statement
❖ Body Paragraph One Topic Sentence
❖ Support used and references
❖ Body Paragraph Two Topic Sentence
❖ Support used and references
❖ Body Paragraph Three Topic Sentence
❖ Support used and references
❖ Conclusion
❖ Comparison/Contrast Markers and Transitions

REAL-WORLD EXAMPLE 2 FOR ANALYSIS
Read the following essay and complete the analysis questions that follow it.

Similarities between Soichiro Honda and Steve Jobs

"Only those who attempt the absurd will achieve the impossible"(Escher). These encouraging words from an author of Drawing Hands, M. Escher, give an idea that whenever people take action, they should not be afraid of a failure and keep making it. Tons of people have a strong desire to succeed in their career and want to acquire a prestige. However, people are faced with a reality that not all people can grasp a chance to be success no matter how they struggle. Among that competitive people, there are two founders who achieved a remarkable success: Steve Jobs who launched a computer company called Apple and Soichiro Honda who launched out a motorcycle company called Honda. Both of them have been known all over the world and created an innovation on their each fields. While Steve Jobs and Soichiro Honda have succeeded in totally different fields, they have unexpected similarities: a great connection with people who are in workplace, an immeasurable influence, and attitude toward failures.

The first surprising similarity between Jobs and Honda is their great connection with people who are in workplace. Both Jobs and Honda had an essential business partner launching out the company. When it comes to Apple, people usually associate with Jobs as everything of Apple; however, there is a man working with Jobs behind the huge success. The man is Jonathan Ive. Those who are close to Apple regard Ive as a person who change the way people think about design. Ive is really relentless, so he has never compromised on making good stuff; as a result, Ive has created lots of creative products with Jobs such as iPhone and iPod. Jobs and Ive have been unseparable since they met in the mid 1990s. People at Apple mention Jobs and Ive as "Jives" because they are always together even in the company dining room. Leander Kahney, the author of Inside Steve's Brain, says, "Steve's relationship with Jony Ive is very symbiotic." It literally means that Jobs needs Ive and Ive needs Jobs; furthermore, it would not have been possible to succeed without each of them. On the other hand, Honda had an unseparable partner as well as Jobs had, named Takeo Fujisawa. Fujisawa was a co-funder of the company, yet he was not only the co-funder but also a manager. In fact, Honda did not get involved in a management of the company at all in spite of his post, president, since he only focused on working on a new development with technicians. Therefore, Fujisawa took over the management and was essential for Honda to flourish the company. It kept a great balance between Honda and Fujisawa by separating their professionals. Honda and Fujisawa have been rumored that there is discord between them; nevertheless, according to Honda Myth, "In Honda circles, Fujisawa was referred to as "Roppongi" after his home in Roppongi, Minato ward; likewise Honda was "Nishiochiai" thanks to his Nishiochiai address in Shinjuku ward"(10). With this reference, it is assumed that both Honda and Fujisawa had an excellent respect to each other. Not only did Jobs and Honda have the essential partner, but also they kept great relationship with their employees. Jobs and Honda had unique technics and leadership in order to lead their employees. Jobs often allowed the employees making mistakes and did not blame them because of the mistakes; therefore, the employees could take action confidently. In Honda's case, he tried to understand a point of view of his employees as much as possible. Moreover, he regarded ideas from the employees as possible alternative plans instead of condemning them; hence, the employees could feel less pressure to propose new ideas.

In addition to a great connection with people who are in workplace, Jobs and Honda have another similarity, which is an immeasurable influence. Both of Jobs and Honda influenced their companies on immeasurable scale. Jobs has once taken the responsibility for the downturn of Apple and resigned. After Jobs was expelled, he launched a new company called NEXT and purchased Pixar, which was bought by Disney. Anyway, while Jobs struggled with running NEXT, Apple's management fell into a death spiral as well. A business article in WIRED states, "By early 1997 it had just 3.3 per cent of the personal computer market and its stock was down to $14 a share"(Rose). Clearly, the situation of Apple got worse gradually after Jobs was expelled. Because of this, Jobs was drawn back to Apple and invented iPod and iMac. In general, it is not usual for a big company that only resignation of the president affects the result of itself badly. This incident revealed the immeasurable influence of Jobs for Apple. Likewise, a same issue occurred in Honda's company. When he was 67 years old, he decided to resign the company because he thought he could not follow the development of technical innovation anymore; however, even though he retired the company, he has been a symbol of it. When it comes to Honda, public always associated with the previous president, Soichiro Honda. Nevertheless, right after Honda's death, the management of the company got worse as well as Apple. During the bad situation, a president at that time, Nobuhiko

Kawamoto, told his employees that they have to forget about the previous president, Honda. The company needs to become a normal company. This Kawamoto's declarant shows how Honda influenced the company strongly. Furthermore, Jobs and Honda influenced public people. Both of them have peculiar way of thinking and public people take their thought into own life. For example, Jobs shared his faith at Stanford Graduation Speech, "Stay hungry. Stay foolish." This phrase becomes famous all over the world, and many public people try to live up to it.

Although great connection with employees and their immeasurable influence are important similarities, Jobs and Honda share an impressive attitude toward failures. People often have negative feelings toward a failure and tend to be afraid of making them. Yet, Jobs and Honda have made the uncountable number of failures in the process of success. For example, as mentioned above, Jobs was expelled from Apple. This must be his ultimate failure in his entire life; however, Jobs stated unexpected words that dismissal from Apple was the most inspiring and best incident for him. Afterwards, he launched out NEXT and owned Pixar. Jobs continued that if he did not leave Apple, Pixar would not have existed and Toy Story would not have been created. Jobs took advantage of the failure and has not given up working because he knew that failure is essential to succeed. Similarly, Honda was also willing to make failures. Honda has remarked, "Success represents the 1% of your work which results from the 99% that is called failure." Being afraid of making failures restrains people from success. Not only did Jobs and Honda simply keep making failures, but also they learned a lot from what they did. Commonly, once people made failures, they did not reflect why they made, but Jobs and Honda analyzed the failure completely. For example, Jobs made a new iPod shuffle, which does not have any buttons. It looked more simple and stylish that it used to be; however, the way of controlling was too complicated, so he realized that too simple lose usefulness. On the other hand, Honda also made lots of failures in the process of making a product. In order to create even one type of car engines, Honda made approximately 100 failures. He changed something little by little and kept changing until he reached the end. Honda thought that when stop thinking, it is time to quit the job. This thought can be applied to anybody who works and can inspire people.

The two successful leaders, Steve Jobs and Soichiro Honda, have surprising similarities: a great connection with people who are in workplace, an immeasurable influence, and attitude toward failures. Through the search of two of them, one common ultimate faith comes up with that both Jobs and Honda loved what they were doing. No matter what and when they faced with difficulties, they could overcome these difficulties because they had strong affection toward their job. Needless to say, every human being wanted to do what they want to do; however, not all people actually achieved dreams. Therefore, people always live in between their desire and reality and need to juggle with the internal conflict. No one knows a right way, but every way can be the best.

Works cited

Escher, M. C. "Drawing Hands" 1948. 26 July 2012

Honda, Soichiro "The interview with TV producer" 30 July 2012

Jobs, Steve "Speech at Stanford Graduation Ceremony" 12 June 2005. 30 July 2012

Kahney, Leander "Inside Steve's Brain" 17 April 2008 Web. 30 July 2012

Masaaki, Sato "The Honda Myth" 19 December 2006 Web. 30 July 2012

Rose, Frank "The End of Innocence: What Happened After Apple Fired Steve Jobs" Wired.com Web. 24 August 2011. 30 July 2012

Sydell, Laula "The Symbiotic Relationship Of Steve Jobs And Jonathan Ive" Npr.com Web. 30 December 2010. 30 July 2012

ANALYSIS
Now that you have read the sample essay, read it again and identify the following parts.

❖ Thesis Statement
❖ Body Paragraph One Topic Sentence
❖ Support used and references
❖ Body Paragraph Two Topic Sentence
❖ Support used and references
❖ Body Paragraph Three Topic Sentence
❖ Support used and references
❖ Conclusion
❖ Comparison/Contrast Markers and Transitions

WRITING BREAK 6 - Summary and Paraphrase (Avoiding plagiarism)

Why do students copy from the text directly?
How do you stop yourself from doing this?

The following paragraph is from a book titled *Swimming and Diving* by David A. Armbruster, Robert H. Allen, and Hobert S. Billingsley.

The first book on swimming was written by Nicolas Wynmann, a German professor of languages, in 1538. A more scientific treatise was later written by Thevenot, a Frenchman, in a book entitled *The Art of Swimming*. The method Thevenot describes resembles closely that which we now call the breaststroke. Although the breaststroke was not adapted to speed swimming, it had many advantages which caused it to remain popular. The stroke gave the swimmer unobstructed forward vision and permitted more freedom for natural breathing. Stroking the arms under the surface prevented splashing the swimmer's face. The stroke thius gave the simmer a feeling of stability, even in rough water. The pioneers constructed this stroke so well that it established the foundation of all strokes. Two and a half centuries after its origin, this method of swimming retains its original characteristics. It is still the most sea-worthy of all our modern strokes.

Let's say that you want to include some of the ideas in this paragraph in your own paper, but you must do it without plagiarizing. In other words, you must not use another person's words or ideas without giving that person credit. In writing, you have plagiarized if you lead a reader to believe that the *words* or *ideas* are yours when they are not. If you used the following sentence in your paper, it would be plagiarism:

The breaststroke is the most sea-worthy of all our modern strokes.

Can you see that it is plagiarism? Find this sentence in the paragraph above on swimming. How much of the sentence is identical to the original sentence?

How then can you as a dedicated student avoid plagiarism? Let's review some skills that will help you.

Quoting

If you want to use the exact words, you must quote. To do this, you must use quotation marks. These are most commonly seen in dialogs because they mark exactly what a person said.

Lupe exclaimed, "Arash is a champion swimmer!"

Let's go back to the swimming sentence above. To correct the plagiarized swimming sentence, you could do the following:

The breaststroke "is the most sea-worthy of all our modern strokes."

Sometimes when quoting, you find yourself in grammatical trouble and you need to change the grammar of the quotation in order to fit your sentence correctly. However, you can't just change someone else's grammar, can you? Look at the example below:

One advantage of the breaststroke is that "stroking the arms under the surface prevented splashing the swimmer's face."

As you can see, the tenses in this sentence are now inconsistent. To incorporate the quotation into the sentence correctly, the grammar must be changed:

One advantage of the breaststroke is that "stroking the arms under the surface prevent[s] splashing the swimmer's face."

The brackets [] indicate that you have changed the original text. Notice that it is a very simple and small change. Nothing to big or complex should be changed if you are quoting directly.

In addition to substituting and adding, there may be times when you need to *delete* part of a word in order to maintain correct grammar.

Today, the breaststroke "had many advantages which caused it to remain popular."

Today, the breaststroke "ha[s] many advantages which [cause] it to remain popular."

Exercise
1. Correct the sentence below.

Swimming has had a long history. The first book on swimming "was written by Nicolas Wynmann, a German professor of languages, in 1538."

2. Complete the sentence below by using a quotation from the paragraph on the breaststroke.

The breaststroke provided the swimmer with _____

_____

3. Correct the problem with the following sentence.

The breaststroke allows the swimmer to "feeling of stability, even in rough water."

_____

_____

Ellipsis
If you leave out part of a sentence in a quotation, you should indicate the part you have omitted by using three periods (ellipsis).

One advantage of the breaststroke is that it provides swimmers with "unobstructed forward vision . . . and more freedom for natural breathing."

Embedded Quotation
At times you will need to quote sentences that have quotations within them. These are called embedded quotations and are surrounded by single quotation marks.

Suppose you are writing about the problem of bears wandering through Valencia. In The Daily News of December 2nd, 2001, you find an article discussing the city council's action to drug bears caught within city limits. You want to include the following in your paper:

Valencia Mayor John Michaels was shouted down at the council meeting by chants of "Keep the bears loose!" led by Lilian Ortega, head of VABA, Valencia Against Bear Abuse.

If you want to include the entire sentence, the quotation marks around the chant *Keep the bears loose* must be changed to single quotation marks.

The conflict between opposing sides of this issue escalated when "Valencia Mayor John Michaels was shouted down at the council meeting by chants of 'Keep the bears loose!' led by Lilian Ortega, head of VABA, Valencia Against Bear Abuse."

Block Quotation

You will sometimes want to quote a written text of more than one sentence. When you do, you must do the following:

1. Single-space the entire quotation
2. Indent on both sides of the quotation
3. Do not use quotation marks
4. Place the author's name(s) and page number after the final period in parentheses.

Example:

While competitive diving has become one of the most popular of Olympic sports, few know about its origins.

> Competitive diving is an outgrowth of aerial acrobatics and tumbling. . . . Feats of diving have been recorded as early as 1871, when divers were reported to have plunged from London Bridge and other high places. . . . The first recorded diving competition took place in England in 1905. (Ambruster, Allen, and Billingsley 11).

Citation

A citation is a source. It gives specific credit to someone else for his or her words or ideas. A citation or reference gives the name of the original author. There are two types of citations – parenthetical and complete.

A parenthetical citation is placed in the paper, immediately following the quotation or idea. It contains the author's last name(s) and the page number(s).

A more scientific treatise was written by Thevenot, a Frenchman, in a book entitled *The Art of Swimming"* (Ambruster, Allen, and Billingsley 1).

A complete citation comes at the end of the paper where you will have a References Page or Works Cited list. This is not the same as a bibliography. A Reference List includes all the works cited in your paper; a bibliography is a list of all the works used in your research, but not necessarily cited in your paper.

Complete citations can be difficult and confusing because, unfortunately, there is more than one accepted style for complete citations. Different academic disciplines use different styles.

Citations and Quotations

You must support the points you make in your paper with outside sources. You need to alert the reader when you are using such sources. In addition to parenthetical citations, you can also put an author's name right in the sentence.

Garinger points out that despite modern scientific evidence, "the controversy over water monsters continues" (15).

What is the name of the author in the sentence above?
What page is the quotation taken from?
Where would the reader find the name of the book the quotation was taken from?

Look at all the other verbs you can use:

According to Garinger, "the controversy over . . ." (15)
As Garinger notes, "the controversy over . . ." (15)
        states, "the controversy over . . ." (15)
        believes, "the controversy over . . ." (15)
Garinger observes that "the controversy over . . ." (15)
        argues that "the controversy over . . ." (15)
        explains that "the controversy over . . ." (15)
        suggests that "the controversy over . . ." (15)

Or

Despite modern scientific evidence, the controversy over water monsters continues," observes Garinger (15).

Paraphrasing - or one of the greatest skills for writers to master!

When you are using primary and secondary sources, there may be situations in which you do not want to use the author's exact words:
The author's words may not fit into the grammar of your sentence.
The language might be inappropriate for your paper – it might be too informal.
You may have already quoted the author too much.

DO NOT FILL YOUR PAPER WITH TOO MANY QUOTATIONS. A collection of quotations pasted together is not a good idea for a paper because you are letting other writers do all the work. Rather than using so many quotations, you should use your own ideas and of course, you can paraphrase.

Example:
Another swimming stroke is the breaststroke. In it, swimmers push their arms out from their chests and then bring them back to their sides. The stroke has several advantages: with it, swimmers can see ahead of them, and they can breathe more naturally (Armbruster, Allen, and Billingsley, 1).

Paraphrasing Techniques
Change the words NOT the meaning.

1. Synonyms

College physical education instructors tend to be former athletes.
Parpaphrase: College gym teachers are often ex-athletes.

What are other words of phrases you might use to paraphrase the following quotation?

"Purchasing a previously owned automobile can be a stressful activity."

Purchasing = _____
Previously owned automobile = _____
Stressful = _____
Activity = _____

Paraphrase for the quotation: _____
_____

2. Negatives and Antonyms

Make the verb negative. Use an antonym.

Be careful not to change the meaning of the sentence.

Example: Students saved their money.
Paraphrase: Students didn't spend their money.

Example: I was awake when they returned last night.
Paraphrase: I wasn't asleep when they came home last night.

Write a paraphrase of the sentences below using a negative and an antonym.

1. "The bear entered the city center."
2. "Maricruz was poor, so she spent the night in a youth hostel."
3. "The country lacks the natural resources for large industries."

Sentence Combining

Put together words, phrases, clauses from more than one sentece.

Example: Madonna started her career as a successful singer. Nevertheless, she makes an enormous amount of money as an actor.
Paraphrase: Although Madonna became famous as a singer, she earns vast amounts of money from her acting.

Practice

Paraphrase the quotation below about Madonna by combining the three clauses. Also, use synonyms to help you.

"Madonna maintains her busy acting and singing career. She is frequently seen in nightclubs in Los Angeles, New York, and Paris. Nevertheless, she provides all the love, tenderness, and care that her daughter, Lourdes, needs."

_____

_____

_____

Moving Phrases

It is not enough just to use synonyms, negative forms, and sentence combining when you paraphrase.

Example: "While watching educational TV programs like Sesame Street, many American children under the age of five acquire basic reading skills."

Bad Paraphrase: While viewing instructional TV programs, many U.S. youngsters get educational skills.

Although the writer has used synonyms, the paraphrase is not good – the language is awkward and the structure is identical to the original.

Good Paraphrase: Many preschoolers in the United States gain reading fundamentals by watching educational TV shows.

One technique for changing the grammar is to <u>move phrases</u>, such as prepositional phrases, around.

Example: Last night, during a game in Los Angeles, the Dodgers first baseman hit the umpire with a bad throw in the seventh inning.

Paraphrase: During the seventh inning of the Dodgers game in Los Angeles last night, the Dodgers first baseman made a terrible throw and hit the umpire.

The sentence below has two prepositional phrases. You can easily move them around the sentence without changing the meaning.
Paraphrase the following sentence by moving one or both of the prepositional phrases:

"In the United States, there is a strong need among senior citizens to remain independent:

Paraphrase: _____

Now, write it again using synonyms and/or negative forms.

Paraphrase: _____

Changing Subjects

a. Change Voice

If a sentence has a transitive verb, another paraphrasing technique is to change its voice: you can make passive sentences active, or you can make active sentences passive.

Active: Someone stole my suitcase from the trunk of my car.
Passive Paraphrase: My luggage was stolen from the back of my car.
Passive: The new campus sports stadium was opposed by some student groups.
Active Paraphrase: Some student groups protested the building of a new sports stadium on campus.

Practice

The sentence below contains a passive verb – make it active. Also, reword the entire sentence using paraphrasing techniques.

"Students are taught by teachers never to plagiarize."

---

b. Changing parts of speech

You can effectively paraphrase by changing the part of speech of the subject or verb.

Example: The librarian's help enabled the student to get their library work done.
Paraphrase: The librarian helped the students finish their library assignment.

Practice

Write a paraphrase of the sentence below by making *emotional shock* the subject. Also, use other techniques to make your paraphrase good.

"Fainting can be triggered by an emotional shock such as the sight of blood."

Using Citations with Paraphrasing

When paraphrasing someone else's ideas, it is usually necessary to give a citation. The only time you do not need a citation with a paraphrase is when the information you are paraphrasing is common knowledge. Unfortunately, deciding when something is common knowledge can sometimes be tricky. For example, it is common knowledge to linguists that languages are always changing. Likewise, art historians know that Wassily Kandinsky is considered one of the founders of abstract expressionism. Similarly, what

166

is commonly known to people in the United States may not be known by people from other countries.

1. Names, dates, places – usually considered common knowledge and do not need any citation in your papers. So, if you wrote that George Washington was the first U.S. president, that the United States declared its Independence in 1776, or that Washington, D.C. is the U.S. capital, you would not need to give a citation. Even though you learned this information from other sources, it is considered common knowledge. The knowledge is not a unique idea developed by one or a small group of people, but rather knowledge that many people share.
2. Information shared by members of a culture need not be cited. The idea that Elvis Presley was the king of rock and roll would not need to be cited because, whether it is true or not, it is widely believed in the United States, and people there would not question it.
3. Information that has been referred to in many sources does not require a citation. For example, the fact that the HIV virus is the cause of AIDS does not need to be cited. Though this was discovered through specific research, it has been so widely referred to that it is now common knowledge.
4. Information that is common sense does not need a citation. The fact that you should dress neatly for a job interview is an idea that most people in the world understand from both logic and experience.

Summarizing Points of View
When writing a summary it is important to be accurate. It is also important to understand and convey the author's point of view. Sometimes, there is no point of view or opinion – it is just facts, but often there is:

The fact that professional boxing still exists in this country is a sign of how far we have to go before we can consider ourselves a civilized society. Boxing is a *sport* in which we pay people to hurt each other as badly as they can. Even if they break the rules in this modern gladiator profession, we all "look the other way." If a boxer bites off part of his opponent's ear, he's given a fine of just 10 percent of his salary. And he is only *suspended* from boxing and can't fight for a short period of time. What would happen to a teacher if he or she bit off part of a student's ear?

What is the author's point of view?
In one sentence summarize the author's point of view.

_____

_____

_____

Paraphrase

Now, paraphrase the above paragraph. Notice that paraphrases are much closer in length to the original than summaries are.

_____

_____

_____

_____

NOW SOME REAL PRACTICE

It is now time to really practice the art of summary and paraphrasing. As you have just read about this in the unit, you will have some idea of what a summary is and what a paraphrase is. You should also have grasped what important skills these two things are for essay writers. Sometimes you need to summarize an author's ideas and source them in a paper. You can summarize an entire page into a few sentences. This is a valuable technique. Paraphrasing, remember, is where you re-word something for clarity. An author might be very poetic, or scientific, or poetically scientific and you might feel like paraphrasing his thoughts in a way to make them more accessible.

If after reading the unit, you still feel unsure, please go to this link for a more complete definition. Remember, researching what you are not sure about simply solidifies your learning, so don't be afraid to do that. http://owl.english.purdue.edu/owl/resource/563/01/

PRACTICE STEP ONE
Get into a group of five.

PRACTICE STEP TWO
In the appendix of this text (Appendix F), you will find 5 short stories. These are all famous short stories and you may have read them before.

In your group, each student will read one of the short stories.

PRACTICE STEP THREE
Now, after each of you has read his/her story, the fun can begin. Imagine you are running a newspaper. You must act like all of these stories are true, and that they have come into your group's newsroom today.

Each of you has to argue for your story to be on the front page.
That means you must treat each story as a discussion topic within the group.
Each member will make a case for his/her story.

Why is your story the most important news item of the day?

What makes your story better and worthy of being the headlines?

As a group, you must then decide who made the best case for the story. Who deserves to be on the front page of your pretend newspaper?

Create a list of the most important story to the least important story. Imagine number one is on the front page, and of course number five will be on the back page with the classifieds.

Story	Newspaper Page	Reasons
	Front	
	2	
	3	
	4	
	Back	

Be prepared to present your list of stories to the class with justifications as to your orders.

PRACTICE STEP FOUR - Go to the stories in the Appendix. Step Four is detailed there.

WRITING BREAK 7 - MLA

It is everywhere. It is on your syllabus (probably). It is said by your instructor. It is on the essay guidelines given for your assignments: Use MLA formatting.

What is MLA Style?
Well, that question is probably too big for a writing break, but we will cover the basics – the concept and a little detail. MLA (Modern Language Association) Style is a system of documentation. It is like other systems such as APA and Chicago. It is used for both scholarly manuscripts and research papers.

Why MLA?
Well, that is the same question as why document? The purpose of documenting your sources is:

1. to show respect to where you found your information by including them in your essay;
2. to show you understand the need to honestly share where you found your research and direct people to those sources;
3. to give the reader all the necessary information to find the sources you used.

A style sheet (as it is often called) will provide you with specific instructions in regard to citing information retrieved from books, magazines, newspapers, scholarly journals, and electronic resources. Oddly, the MLA Style Sheet eats up a whole book and not a very thin one. Fortunately, the Internet has made life much easier for all of us.

Below is as brief a guide as you can get and do not be deluded – it does not cover everything (it does not come close to covering everything). It does, however, continue your learning journey in this aspect of academic writing.

Works Cited
This is a detailed alphabetical list of all the works that you cited in your paper. MLA has specific rules and style guidelines for formatting the Works Cited page.

In Your Essay
In-text or parenthetical citations are those that appear in your essay. These are much shorter versions of what appears at the end of the essay because quite honestly, the reader does not want to be interrupted or distracted and so the brief reference to the source is all that is needed.

The reader can get the detailed information from the Works Cited page at the end. As you see, there is a definite connection between the two.

I have a saying, "If it's in the essay, it's at the end and if it's at the end, it's in the essay." I use this to stress to students that if you use a name in your essay, that name needs to be at the end of the essay in the Works Cited page. Similarly, if you have a Works Cited page with ten sources on it, those ten names/sources must be in the essay.

For any style of writing like MLA, you must follow specific rules and instructions when citing information from a source be it a book, a periodical – magazine, journal, newspaper – Website, database. Most students do not find it fun to follow these rules and that is okay; it is not supposed to be fun. Not following the rules, however, is not the answer. This is one of those things that students must do and in some ways, it really is just following the rules. Also, if you collect the information you need as you research, life will also be easier. In addition, academic sources often give you the citation in the appropriate format!

- ❖ Identify the source
- ❖ Collect the information
- ❖ Go to an MLA Stylesheet
- ❖ Note the in-text reference:
- ❖ Note the Works Cited reference:

The examples below follow the seventh edition of MLA Handbook for Writers of Research Papers New York: Modern Language Association of America, 2009.

A Few Examples of citations for books and periodicals

Book:

Peretti, Burton W. Jazz in American Culture. American Ways Series. Chicago: Ivan R Dee, 1997. Print.

How would this look in the text?

It was Peretti who argued for the supremacy of the Jazz movement when others were afraid to do so (31).

The Jazz movement was the supreme form of music in its time (Peretti 31).

Article from a magazine:

Taylor, Chris "Microsoft's Future" Time 17 April 2000: 55. Print.

How would this look in the text?

Taylor (55) maintains that Microsoft is well-placed to face the future of the technological world.

It has been maintained that Microsoft is well-placed to face the future of the technological world (Taylor 55).

Documenting information from the Internet

When citing information from the Internet, you MUST cite;

WHO create the information
WHERE the information came from
WHEN you accessed the information
TITLE of the site or page (top left-hand corner of the screen)
SITE CREATION DATE if available

Here are two examples of how to cite Web sites, both accessed on September 1, 2009:

Academic Web site:

Epstein, Joan F., and Joseph C. Gfroerer. "Heroin Abuse in the United States." OAS Working Paper August 1997. Web. 01 Sept. 2009

How would this look in the text?

Epstein and Gfroerer provide an outstanding portrayal of just what kinds of heroin abuse take place in the United States.

The incomprehensibly high levels of heroin abuse in the United States have concrete, if surprising, causes and roots (Epstein and Gfroerer).

Personal Web site:

"John Gotti and the Gambino Family." Web. 01 Sept. 2009.

In-text citation: ("John Gotti")

Documenting information from the Library's subscription databases

Many students rightly use the resources made available through their libraries. Libraries subscribe to certain databases such as ProQuest Direct. If using these sources, you need to note the following:

PUBLICATION in which information appeared originally
NAME of the database used
DATE you accessed the database

Examples:

Watson, Russell "Sending in the troops." Newsweek 31 May 1999: 36.   ProQuest Direct. Web. 01 Sept. 2009.

How would this look in the text?

In-text citation: (Watson)

"Norma Jean Baker." International Dictionary of Films and Filmmakers, Volume 3: Actors and Actresses. St. James Press, 1996. Biography Resource Center. Web. 01 Sept. 2009.

In-text citation: ("Norma Jean Baker")

Essentially, there is no EASY MLA guide or QUICK MLA guide. The whole system is laden with rules and regulations that cannot be condensed into two lines. That being said, the above breakdown should give you a beginning insight into the concept of citations and the formatting required. The good news is that there are many resources out there to help you.

---

1. Your college library and your college librarians and your college library website.
2. Any college library website from Cornell to Purdue!
3. Online Citation Makers (but they can be a little unreliable and still need checking) such as refworks.com, easybib.com – Just Google MLA citation maker.
4. Two of my favorites:
   a. http://www.ccc.commnet.edu/mla/index.shtml
   b. http://owl.english.purdue.edu/owl/resource/747/01/

How do you get better at MLA? There is only one way and that is to practice. Therefore. let's do that now. Find your last essay and analyze it by answering the questions in the table below. You can use this table for any of your essays in this class and in future classes. Some of the questions are yes/no but many of them require more thoughtful responses.

#	Question	Yes/No
	Do you have a Works Cited page as the final page in your essay?	
	Is your Works Cited Page formatted correctly? Is it double-spaced, alphabetical by author, indented etc.?	
	Do you have references **in** your essay?	
	For each reference, is there a matching entry in the Works Cited Page? Be very systematic and careful in your checking and counting.	
	Organize your sources by Type. Choose one of the types – books, Internet, database – and go to one of the MLA websites suggested above or your own favorite and compare the formatting for both in-text and the Works Cited page – do they match? What is different?	
	Choose another type and repeat #5	
	What weaknesses and strengths do you notice about your use of MLA? How can you improve?	
	What MLA-related questions do you still have? Where might you find answers to those questions?	

WRITING MODULE 5
THE ARGUMENT ESSAY

This is a big topic. From Greece to Rome to the Founding Fathers and beyond, the argument has shaped policy, philosophy and the very essence of understanding by rigorous examination, claims, warrants and refutation. If you can organize your arguments around the principles taught in this chapter, you will never again have to answer a question with a simple yes or no. It is the great pride of intellect and the sad decline of simplicity in your life, so bid the simple life farewell if you intend to master this form of rhetoric.

Years back this essay used to be called the research paper until the English Composition teachers got together and decided that most students were afraid of the word research and much preferred the word argument. For the most part, an argument paper is a research paper that sounds slightly less intimidating. Now the veil is off, and you know that this paper is going to require the most effort in terms of research and understanding of a topic from every angle. I'd like to give you the basics before we start looking in depth at the function of each paragraph in this new mode of rhetoric.

ARGUMENT ESSAY STRUCTURE

Up until now we have been doing five-paragraph essays; however, the argument essay adds a sixth paragraph: the counter argument and refutation.

Look at the classical style of argument presented on the next page.

I.   Introduction

    a. Opening

    b. Summary of issue

    c. Background information

    d. Thesis

II.   Appeals and evidence for argument one

    a. Appeals based on ethos, pathos and or logos.

    b. Appeals based on stats, examples or authoritative texts

III. Appeals and evidence for argument two

    a. Appeals based on ethos, pathos and or logos.

    b. Appeals based on stats, examples or authoritative texts

IV.   Appeals and evidence for argument three

    a. Appeals based on ethos, pathos and or logos.

    b. Appeals based on stats, examples or authoritative texts

V.   Counter argument and refutation

VI.   Conclusion

    a. Review of key points

    b. Recommendations

    c. Restatement of thesis

Each numbered section above is a paragraph in an argument essay. We will start by discussing the differences between this paper and all of the rest that you have produced up until now.

THESIS

The key word in an argument paper is "should." This presents your idea of how a problem should be solved. The common model is below:

To solve the problem of _____, they should do _____, _____ and

_____.

Here is an example thesis.

The three main ways that the state should fight poverty are with improved education, improved enforcement of drug laws, and a repeal of all gambling licenses including the state lottery system.

This thesis will be expanded in the body paragraphs, but the essence of my thesis is that if people are smarter, less able to get intoxicated, and less able to gamble that there will be less poverty. Notice how all of the changes are controlled by one entity: the state. I am organizing around a central mode of change because it makes my proof easier.

Body Paragraphs - Counter Argument and Refutation

Most of the body paragraphs are the same as before. However, there is a difference. Look back at the classical outline and notice that the fourth body paragraph is different. In this paragraph, the writer takes on the personality of a person on the other side of the issue. This is to show that you are an educated writer who is aware that there are multiple arguments and sides to an issue and that you considered the other side before putting forth your position. In other words, you must take the key arguments against your own position and present them. After presenting them, you point out why they are incorrect, false, erroneous, weak, mistaken etc; you refute them. Please note that this does not mean that you simply tear down your paper. What you are doing makes your paper stronger, more informed, and thus, more credible. In short, this process when done correctly actually strengthens your paper. Take the items point by point following the model thesis from above. I might begin my counter argument and refutation paragraph like this.

EXAMPLE

Many people believe that education is only necessary for a certain class of jobs and that anyone who works hard will get ahead. (counters my point that education is important) However, with the expanding technology sector where 90 percent of the jobs require a college degree and a shrinking industrial sector where less than 15 percent of the workers are expected to have a college education, one can easily see that the key to employment is education. Another criticism of education is that it steals productive years from a person entering the workplace. This is not the case; a study was done on the lifetime earning potential of people –

Notice the following:

1. The counterargument is not long – it is merely a presentation of the other side.
2. The counterargument is followed by a refutation.
3. The refutation is introduced by a transition word or phrase - however, this is not the case.
4. The refutation is significantly longer than the counterargument.

Thus the counterargument presents the other side, but ultimately I showed how my argument was stronger by immediately refuting the claims of the other side. Your goal in this essay is to counter and refute all three points in one paragraph. Transition from point to point and don't worry if the paragraph is a little bit longer than the other body paragraphs.

RESEARCH OBJECTIVES

Argument essays require at least three unique sources per paragraph. Do not repeat the same source. Find three different supports for each argument you make in the paper. Do not use Encyclopedia as sources; I should not have to mention this, but they are collections of general knowledge, and you need to find an actual author to quote if you want to include his or her ideas in your paper. Look at easybib.com or the MLA chapter of this book for formatting help on your Works Cited page.

First Argument

Because we are in class together we will start off small and not go into something emotional that reflects your personal views. The best way to do this is to choose a book or even a short story and start with at timeline. Go from the beginning of the book to the end and trace the characters ups and downs in love, prosperity, anger, or happiness. Look at the example below. You could also do this for a movie like Groundhog Day which you may have covered earlier in this book.

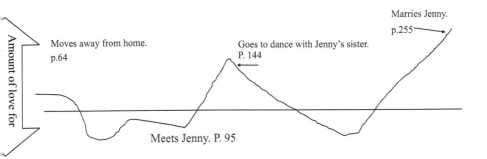

Marries Jenny.
p.255

Moves away from home.
p.64

Goes to dance with Jenny's sister.
P. 144

Meets Jenny. P. 95

Amount of love for

EMAIL OR WEB SPECIAL

Use a book or short story you have been studying in class. If you haven't been reading the same book go to barleby.com, gutenburg.com or readprint.com and find a story that the entire class can read before the next meeting. Divide the class into two groups. One group is going to track the prosperity of the character using a graph like the example on the previous page. The other group is going to track the character from the point of view of his relationships (love, friendship, whatever you choose) with others.

Each group will choose the graphs from their group that look the most different and their creators will present them side by side. The class should be prepared to argue over their choices and present specifics from the story that back up their position.

IN-CLASS PRACTICE

Now we will move into a practice that will help you understand the importance of each body paragraph in an argument essay. Take a blank piece of paper. Divide your paper into six sections, one for each paragraph in an argument answer. Under each section, answer the following questions.

Introduction

What is an introduction? How should it start?
What is important to remember about the thesis of an argument paper? Give an example of an argument paper thesis.

Body Paragraph 1

Define a body paragraph. What is the purpose of a body paragraph in an argument paper? What are the elements of a body paragraph that are expected? What are the expectations within this class?

Every argument has two sides; are you supposed to talk about both in the body paragraph of an argument essay?

Body Paragraph 2

The topic is that high school students should wear school uniforms. Find research to back this up and write it down here along with the correct MLA format for the source.

Body Paragraph 3

The topic is: The government should raise the minimum wage. Find a source to support this and write it down here along with a transition that introduces a second reason for the need to raise the minimum wage.

Counter-Argument and Refutation Paragraph 4

This is the paragraph that is new to your papers. What is it? How do you write it? What are the rules about writing a counter argument paragraph?

What would the counter arguments be for a paper that claims that America should "go green." What are the refutations?

Define the paragraph first; then provide examples given the topic above.

Conclusion

How do you write an effective conclusion to an argument paper? What does it mean to restate the thesis? List the different ways that you can end an argument paper. As always, research before you write down your answers. Some people say that a good conclusion is like a pyramid. What do you think that means?

Last Research Assignment

ALONE

There are three topics below. Your job is to narrow each into a thesis statement appropriate for an argument essay.

IN PAIRS

Exchange thesis statements and make comments. Work together to choose the strongest thesis for each other.

GROUPS OR CLASS

When everyone is done, present your strongest thesis statement to the class. It is the job of other students to argue against your thesis.

As students present arguments against your thesis, you must address each concern expressed. This will be much like the counterargument paragraph in your final essay. Show your peers how their concerns are valid, but how your position is stronger than theirs. Use research to support your points.

Your instructor will direct you on whether to continue this activity in groups or as a class. It can be done effectively as a large group, as a carousel with students rotating around each thesis, or online in a discussion board.

Topic 1 The Economy in the United States

Example:

There are three things that Obama should do to promote job growth in America: Blah, blah and blah.

Your thesis:

Student Response:

Topic 2 Foreign Wars

Example:

*America must _____, _____, and _____
to end the violence in Darfur.*

Your thesis:

Student Response:

Topic 3 Health in a New Age

Example:

*The essential programs of preventative care that should be introduced into every
HMO in America are program one, program two, and program three.*

Your thesis:

Student Response:

WRITING PRACTICE

Write a counterargument-refutation paragraph based on the primary
arguments presented by your peers.

Refutation Research

Refute each of the contrary student responses to your argument using research from books, journals, or articles. Do NOT use websites unless there is an author attached to the text on the website. Each letter, ABC, should be a piece of support that proves that the counterarguments against your paper are weaker than your central argument.

Topic Thesis:

Counterargument 1 from Class:

A. Refutation:

Counterargument 2 from Class:

B. Refutation:

Counterargument 3 from Class:

C. Refutation

Take the notes/outlines from above and turn it into a coherent and unified paragraph. Bring your paragraph to class for peer and instructor feedback.

Argument Uses All You Have Learned

The joy of the argument paper is that it uses any rhetorical mode that it can to make the argument clear and convincing. This means that the modes you have been learning about throughout this test - comparison, contrast, cause, effect, even classification - can be used in an argument paper to prove your point. If you are arguing about school uniforms, maybe a comparison of achievement scores between two schools (one which mandates uniforms and the other which doesn't) could help prove your point. Maybe some of the psychological effects on students could be analyzed to show how students are affected by their wardrobe in school. A brief classification of wardrobe in the standard public school could convince people that uniforms are the answer. Do not be afraid to apply all of the techniques you have learned to convince a reader that your point of view is strong. Students have notoriously strong minds, and coupled with the right tools for expression and rigorous defense, those notorious ideas will go farther and formidable arguments will be introduced into class from all sides. In this kind of environment, one cannot help but learn and excel.

Well, I could now argue with great efficacy that you have crossed a bridge and can now tackle writing assignments in your college composition classes and other subject classes with confidence and with knowledge of structure, coherence, unity, support, research, and content. Congratulations! You should feel proud of yourself.

Extend the Bridge

Appendix A

Paragraphs

Some students need a brief refresher on the components of a paragraph. Here is a simple version.

Key Parts of a Paragraph
Topic Sentence

This is what expresses the main idea of the paragraph. It shows the direction and writer's attitude toward the subject. It gives the reader some idea of where the paragraph is going. The topic sentence can be preceded by "introductory sentences" if the topic needs some background; in a paragraph of 300 words, however, the introductory sentences should not be longer than the supporting points, so be careful how you use them.

Supporting Points

Your paragraphs will typically contain at least three supporting points. The purpose of each supporting point is to support the main idea. These points, therefore, are the key ideas around which your paragraph is basing its strength.

Details

The supporting point identifies the key point but it is the details which do the work of explaining and adding validity.

Concluding Sentence

This is the sentence which brings the paragraph to a close. Many books tell you to rephrase your topic sentence and this leads to repetition, but usually you can do better than that by using different vocabulary and grammar and by adding another element like a suggestion or a warning.

As the topic sentence is the first sentence that the reader reads, it needs to identify the topic of the paragraph.

This is the main idea of your paragraph.

The topic sentence:
- ❑ Introduces the topic

- ❏ States the main idea – the controlling idea
- ❏ Is the most general sentence

Examples of Topic Sentences

Topic   controlling idea
<u>Leaving the family home</u> is a <u>traumatic experience for some college students.</u>

controlling idea   Topic
<u>The most exciting and important part of a youth's life</u> is leaving the family home.

How do you write a topic sentence?
The difficulty of writing topic sentences is not really the writing of them but the narrowing of a greater topic. Let's look at an example.

Broad Topic: College
This means that you are going to talk about college in general. That could be okay, but it is often better to narrow that down a little. Do you mean a four-year college like a university or a two-year college like community college? Do you have a specific college in mind or do you really want to say something about college in general? Do you mean college in general or do you want to talk about college life or a college education?
Do you see how the one term of "college" leads us to many questions which can help narrow down what we want to write about? So if the instructor gives you an assignment which reads, - <u>Write a paragraph about college?</u> - You have a lot of freedom to explore that word and what you want to say.

Narrower topic: College of the Canyons

That is pretty easy, isn't it? Now you need to take a broad topic and narrow it. No sentence writing just now; simply narrow a larger topic to a more manageable one that could be the main topic of a paragraph.

On the following pages are some sample paragraphs with analysis and outlining exercises.

SAMPLE PARAGRAPH ONE

In Los Angeles life without a car is not only unimaginable but also impractical. First and foremost, the lack of an effective public transportation system makes private means of travel non-negotiable. Santa Clarita is a perfect example. The bus system exists but is extremely limited in frequency and route. As a result, being a regular bus user requires a flexible schedule; unfortunately, most people's routines are dictated by work and school making flexibility a luxury. In addition, if a person's workplace or school is not in Santa Clarita, it is necessary to transfer buses. Of course, this only adds time and inconvenience to the trip. In fact, it can take up to three hours to get from the Santa Clarita Valley to the San Fernando Valley depending on when you need to travel. This is a trip which takes around twenty minutes by car. Moreover, if Los Angeles is the destination, the bus system is beyond inconvenient. The alternative is the Metrolink but like the bus, the Metrolink suffers from a limited schedule. It is also relatively expensive at eleven dollars for a round trip. The lack of an alternate transportation system is a strong argument for the value of the automobile, but so is the physical make-up of the city of Los Angeles. It is often noted that Los Angeles has no real city center like New York or Washington D.C. do. This means that businesses, stores, housing, and entertainment are often located beyond walking distance from each other. Interestingly, it is also often said that nothing in Los Angeles is more than twenty minutes away. Of course, the missing part of this statement is "by car". In order to move around this city and take advantage of all that it has to offer, some means of transportation is essential. In order to move around the city freely, nothing is more beneficial than a car. The lack of public transportation alternatives and the physicality of Los Angeles lead to one more advantage of the automobile, namely economics. An effective public transportation system saves the consumer money and for this, the consumer makes certain concessions in convenience, but the system in Los Angeles is neither convenient nor cheap. In contrast, buying, running, and maintaining a car in Los Angeles is relatively inexpensive. The initial purchase price may seem high, but there are many great financial opportunities on new and used cars. More important is the fact that gas prices are unarguably low, even today, especially when compared to many other developed countries where a car owner can expect to pay on average of six dollars a gallon. This reduces the overall expense of a car so much so that the automobile has become a part of the average Los Angelean's routine. It is, therefore, hard to imagine life in this sprawling city without the means to navigate it at will. Fortunately, it is unnecessary for people her to even have to try because nowhere is the dependence on the automobile so evident as in Los Angeles.

ANALYSIS

What do you think the assignment for the above paragraph was?

Find the following:
- ❖ The topic sentence
- ❖ The Three Supporting Points
- ❖ The Details (examples, facts etc.)
- ❖ Transitions introducing the Supporting Points

Do you think the paragraph is coherent?

Coherent means organized and logical. If yes, what makes it coherent? Identify specifically why you think the paragraph is coherent. If no, why not? Where exactly do you think it is not well put together or logically organized?

Do you think the paragraph is unified?

Unified means everything is on topic – the supporting points support the topic sentence and the details support the supporting points! If yes, identify how each point supports the ideas. If no, identify where the paragraph goes astray (off topic).

Outline

Complete an outline of the paragraph

Topic Sentence: _____

_____

Transition + SP 1: _____

_____

    Details:
- ❖
- ❖
- ❖

Transition + SP 2: _____

_____

    Details:
- ❖
- ❖
- ❖

Transition + SP 3: _____

_____

    Details:

- ❖
- ❖
- ❖

Concluding Sentence _____

SAMPLE PARAGRAPH TWO

John Macintosh, and not Peter Blane, is undeniably the most appropriate choice for the role of James Bond. First of all, unlike the other actors, John has a variety of movie experience as both supporting actor and lead actor. Although Peter has also been the lead in two movies, they were student films and not professional ones. Moreover, John has had experience in action movies. Not only was he in *The Matrix*, he was also in *2Fast2Furious*. John's experience in action movies is not the only reason he will be the best James Bond. John is, in fact, very athletic and the role of James Bond requires great physicality. In contrast to Peter, John plays in ice-hockey, soccer, and tennis leagues. Admittedly, Peter is very physically strong; he does wrestling and can water-ski. This may seem to make him John's equal, but this would be a mistake. John is far more versatile than Peter. While John can run, swim, cycle, skate, and is a black-belt in karate, Peter can only lift heavy things and be pulled along in the water by someone else. Another important difference between John and Peter is John's linguistic abilities. James Bond is a spy and can speak several languages. Moreover, he must be able to blend in to his environment. John speaks English, Spanish, Italian, German, Farsi, and Japanese. No matter where the movie is set – Europe, Asia, the Middle East – John will fit. Peter has only mastered English and Spanish. In addition, John is very talented with accents. He can imitate a New Yorker, a Texan, an Englishman, a Russian, or an Asian. He has even trained with Dr. Lev Bubenheffel, the famous accent coach. His abilities and experience in accents outweigh those of Peter. Last, but certainly not least, is the most important difference. John is extremely good-looking and even looks a little bit like the Bonds that went before him (Sean Connery, Pierce Brosnan, even Roger Moore). At six foot three inches, John is taller than Peter by at least three inches. His black hair and brown eyes make him look dark and a little mysterious, even unpredictable. Even though Peter has the same hair and eye color, he doesn't have the same high cheekbones that give John a look of intelligence. Furthermore, James Bond is a charming man and that means his smile attracts many people, both men and women. In his picture, Peter has a fun smile. He looks like he might be your best friend or neighbor. John's smile, on the other hand, is a mixture of seriousness and amusement. The corners of his mouth turn up slightly, so you know he is smiling but he doesn't look completely involved. He looks like he has more important things to think about, like protecting government secrets or saving the world from nuclear disaster. In short, John's experience, looks, physical abilities, and linguistic talents are superior to those Peter's and make him the perfect choice as the next James Bond.

ANALYSIS

What do you think the assignment for the above paragraph was?

Find the following:
   ❖ The topic sentence
   ❖ The Three Supporting Points
   ❖ The Details (examples, facts etc.)
   ❖ Transitions introducing the Supporting Points

Do you think the paragraph is coherent?

Coherent means organized and logical. If yes, what makes it coherent? Identify specifically why you think the paragraph is coherent. If no, why not? Where exactly do you think it is not well put together or logically organized?

Do you think the paragraph is unified?

Unified means everything is on topic – the supporting points support the topic sentence and the details support the supporting points! If yes, identify how each point supports the ideas. If no, identify where the paragraph goes astray (off topic).

Outline

Complete an outline of the paragraph

Topic Sentence: _____

_____

Transition + SP 1: _____

_____

    Details:
- ❖
- ❖
- ❖

Transition + SP 2: _____

_____

    Details:
- ❖
- ❖
- ❖

Transition + SP 3: _____

_____

    Details:

- ❖
- ❖
- ❖

Concluding Sentence _____

APPENDIX B

Outlining

What is outlining? Why should you do it? If you don't get points for the outline, how will it help your grade?

Outlining is like ice hockey. Nobody wakes up one morning and decides to play hockey (my apologies to the Canadian audience). But some people upon being pushed onto the ice become very adept at the sport and grow to love it and the brutal athleticism involved. That's exactly like outlining.

Outlining Structure

One in-depth and useful resource on outlining can be found at: http://papyr.com/hypertextbooks/comp1/outline.htm

Another way to outline is to use Powerpoint. We use this in teaching essay writing by making each slide a paragraph. Powerpoint then has an Outline feature which basically puts your work into that outline format.

In brief, an outline takes the key parts of the essay and presents them for easy reading. An effective outline makes it easy to see what is in your essay.

In Appendix A, there are paragraphs to be outlined if you want some practice.

On the next page is a blank essay outline form. Feel free to use it. Of course, if you are doing an argument essay, this will need an extra paragraph.

Introduction: Hook?

Thesis:

_____

_____

BP I. _____

    A.

        1.
        2.
        3.

    B.

        1.
        2.
        3.

BP II. _____

    A.

        1.
        2.
        3.

    B.

        1.
        2.
        3.

BP III . _____

    A.

        1.
        2.
        3.

    B.

        1.
        2.
        3.

Conclusion:

Restate thesis _____

Final Thoughts:
_____

APPENDIX C

One can learn so much from reading sample essays, so on the following pages are some more for your reading pleasure. Apply the same analysis techniques that you did to your earlier essays to discuss and learn from these samples.

SAMPLE ONE - PLAGIARISM

Plagiarism has become a heated debate over the last decade especially with the concurrent spread of information through the Internet. While the definition of plagiarism is itself a debate, in this context, it is being kept simple and focused meaning the taking of others' ideas and representation of them as one's own. Ashworth, Freewood, & McDonald (2003) maintain that plagiarism assumes personal authorship, creativity, originality, individual ownership, and the idea that knowledge has a history and authors must indeed be recognized. They conclude that plagiarism is a very Western idea. It is of no surprise, therefore, that the major players in the culture-conditioning debate are China and Japan. The culture-conditioning hypothesis (Liu 2005) in which culture is primarily responsible for Asian students plagiarizing and cheating has provoked conflicting research and dissenting opinion in recent years.

At the heart of the debate are the perceived differing cultural values and norms. Dryden (1999) points to differences in concepts of ownership of words and ideas between Japan and the Western educational systems. She argues that social and educational Confucian patterns have persisted into contemporary times. In this idea, knowledge is presumed to be static, something that can be mastered and memorized. If this is indeed the case, then the copying of ideas shows mastery rather than lack of originality. Sowden (2005) also points to the historical with the claim that Chinese academic norms stem from, in part, a very long tradition of reproducing Confucian teachings in civil- servant exams. Being able to reproduce Confucius' words without any citations was considered praiseworthy. Perhaps more significant is the idea that original thinking should be avoided as the student is trained to be a good listener preoccupied with details and correct forms. In a 1993 study of plagiarism in Hong Kong students, Deckert argued for considering the differences in scholarly traditions and specifically the Chinese emphasis on a "close allegiance to a few acknowledged authorities with resulting convergence of perspective and greater social harmony" (p. 132). This is supported by Sowden's observation that in China good students do not challenge their teachers. In a similar vein, in Japan, the complex social-structural relationships of subordinates and superiors (kohei and sempai) limits the originality not only expected but also allowed of students. In a personal interview with Dryden, Morrone from Nagoya University's School of Business puts it best, "In short, one earns a right to develop an opinion slowly and over the course of adulthood"(p. 79).

Culture and society, therefore, are a significant part of this debate. Neither Sowden (2005), nor Dryden (1999), nor Morrone (1996) explicitly state that Asian students' culture tells them that cheating is acceptable. They simply imply. In apparent contradiction, Dryden makes the valid point that in Japan cheating on exams is considered tantamount to sin. When plagiarism is defined, therefore, as cheating, the concept that Asian cultures are pro-cheating cultures is challenged. Buranen (1999), based on studies of Japanese students, purports that plagiarism is cultural but actually denies specific cultural practices leading to plagiarism. Most noticeably, within all of the above arguments in the culture-plagiarism debate is the idea of the collective over the group, often associated with Asian cultures. It is Sapp (2002) that bridges this idea and transitions into the staunch dissenters of cultural responsibility. Sapp cites repeated instances of his Chinese students plagiarizing. He traces the cause of this plagiarism not as something supported by culture and society but as something stemming from the context of his students. While conceding that the Asian concept of group plays a role in this (everyone copied to achieve a high-score on the language test) as well as the idea that in China learning is cooperative, collaborative, and supportive and, therefore, less individualistic than in the West, Sapp only attributes part of this to the collective of the group over the individual. Liu (2005) also questions the fundamental idea that in China group work is encouraged but, unfortunately, offers no clear support of this.

It is Liu (2005) that is the greatest dissenter on this issue. Personal and professional experience ground his argument that cultural conditioning is not the major culprit. Liu maintains that plagiarism is not encouraged by teachers or institutions and that current writing texts address the issue of plagiarism and how it is wrong. Although in essence agreeing with Liu, Sapp (2002) points out a discrepancy between policy in China and actual institutional support. Sowden (2005) also disagrees with Liu's praising of the Chinese government's recent studies and policies to combat plagiarism raising the difficulty of distrusting a government with the current Chinese government's history. Sapp is in accord with Sowden as he attributes his students' plagiarism to being a reflection of the cheating going in society (as well as the world). Sapp repeatedly returns to context and not culture being responsible for plagiarism. Although Sapp and Liu present differing views of the same society and government's attitudes to plagiarism in support of their arguments, they are ultimately on the same side.

A sensitive issue, the notion that plagiarism is culturally driven has provoked interesting discussion while trying to avoid stereotyping. Plagiarism is not limited to nationality – students plagiarize be they American, Chinese, English, or Japanese. Perhaps all those involved in the above debate are correct when they acknowledge (to varying degrees) that plagiarism is about intent. They probably all concur with Sapp (2002) that context is the greatest factor in students plagiarizing. With the advancing of technology, the collective digital culture of the new generation will perhaps transcend the individual targets of specific countries. That being said, maybe the collective over the individual will truly be relevant.

References

Buranen, L. (1999). I wasn't cheating: Plagiarism and cross-cultural mythology. In L. Buranen &. A. M. Roy (Eds.), *Perspectives on plagiarism and intellectual property in a postmodern world*. (pp. 63-74). New York: State University of New York Press.

Deckert, G. D. (1993). Perspectives on plagiarism from ESL students in Hong Kong. *Journal of Second Language Writing, 1993*(2), 131-148.

Dryden, L. M. (1999). A distant mirror or through the looking glass? Plagiarism and intellectual property in Japanese education. In L. Buranen & A. M. Roy (Eds.), *Perspective on plagiarism and intellectual property in a postmodern world*. (pp. 75-86). New York: State University of New York Press.

Liu, D. (2005). Plagiarism in ESOL students: Is cultural conditioning truly the major culprit. *ELT Journal, 59*(3), 234-241.

Ashworth, P., Freewod, M., & Macdonald, R. (2003). The student lifeworld and the meanings of plagiarism. *Journal of Phenomenological Psychology, 34*(3), 257-278.

Sapp, D. A. (2002). Towards and international and intercultural understanding of plagiarism and academic dishonesty in composition: Reflections from the People's Republic of China. *Issues in Writing, 13*(1), 58-79.

Sowden, C. (2005). Plagiarism and the culture of multilingual students in higher education abroad. *ELT Journal, 59*(3), 226-233.

SAMPLE TWO – THE INTERNET (instructor comments included)

"Twenty years ago no one could have imagined the effects the Internet would have: entire relationships flourish, friendships prosper...there's a vast new intimacy and accidental poetry, not to mention the weirdest porn. The entire human experience seems to unveil itself like the surface of a new planet.(J.G. Ballard)" Ballard's comment is an admirably succinct diagnosis of the effects the internet has had on humanity. The internet has had its effect on our relationships, our study habits, our free time, our careers, and even the way we shop. The uses and applications of the internet are so many and varied that most people who have access to it will find at least some use for it, but the true variable in the equation is how much use a given user will find. Some of us hardly use the internet at all, and then, only when its absolutely necessary, while others are constantly connected. Internet users can therefore be separated into three distinct categories, based on how useful a tool the internet is for them. The three groups are: the utilitarian user, the convenience user, and the constantly connected. **– this is unparallel grammatically and also the utilitarian implies purpose, the convenience implies purpose, but the constantly connected implies a state which brings into question your classification principle.**

Even with the vast amount of information and applications available online today in America, there are some users who find only a insignificant amount of use for the internet. These Utilitarian Users have a tendency to gravitate towards the less complicated and less involved processes available, such as e-mail, shopping, travel, and health information. The majority of users will use the internet for all of these uses, and a huge majority of 91 percent will utilize the internet for e-mail purposes (**So are you saying that all users are utilitarian users? Or do you have a relevant point and something that is going to separate utilitarian users because above you said that they did not just use it for email...**), but the trail of statistics leads to a sharp decline in usage for the more complicated uses such as downloading video, with only 18 percent of

200

users accomplishing this task, and 25 percent downloading music. Members of the Utilitarian User group also tend to be older then those in the other subgroups – (*So what age are the members of this group – your explanation got confusing here*). Internet users in the 72-75 year age group are just as likely to use e-mail then any other age group, but far less likely to use the internet for most of its other uses.(*How is this relevant?*)[1] **COHERENCE** The internet is a relatively recent addition to our technology, and it is therefore not surprising that those who have grown up with the internet at there disposal will find more use for it and be more comfortable taking advantage of the more complicated uses –(**How is this relevant to utilitarian users or are you digressing?**) It has, in recent years, become not only easier, but in some cases necessary, to do certain things via the internet, such as sending mail, and travel reservations, and even shopping, (*Give an example of when shopping via the Internet is essential*) which is why these Utilitarian Users will find themselves, even if reluctantly, using the internet for these reasons. They will not, however, use the internet for much else.

Apart from the very basic applications that appeal to the Utilitarian User, there are other, often more complex uses, that will appeal to the Casual User. The Casual User is one who will gain a significant amount of use from the internet by using it to complete everyday tasks that could otherwise be accomplished by traditional means. Applications like online bill paying, banking, and even filling employment applications will be utilized by the Casual User who is, by definition, more comfortable with these more complex tasks then the Utilitarian User. The convenience of online banking is especially appealing, with just over one-third of all adults doing there banking online.[2] It is important to note that the Casual User's tendencies revolve around convenience rather then necessity, like the Utilitarian user, or as an end in itself, like the next group, the Constantly Connected User. *This is a much more focused paragraph; it is also a little*

---

[1] http://www.pewinternet.org/pdfs/PIP_Generations_Memo.pdf

[2] http://www.packagedfacts.com/Online-Retail-Banking-959462/

light on content and research – three sources per paragraph is the requirement, so why do you have only one? Who exactly is the Utilitarian user? You spent lines and lines on age in the previous paragraph; is age not relevant here?

The internet is not only a means for convenience or utility, but a means to entertain, educate, communicate, buy, sell, research, and in all other ways, interact with society on the electronic level. It is the Constantly Connected User that will utilize the internet for all of these applications, not out of convenience or necessity, but out of desire for the unique interactions and experiences offered by the internet. (**(you have to address the name you have given this group – are they indeed constantly connected?**) It is within this group that we find the Web Log, or Blog, authors, the chat room regulars, the hard core gamers, and the pornography enthusiasts (**are these really "constantly connected" users? Can you prove that?**). These applications (*is pornography an application?*) are unique because they are not an internet related means to achieve a reality based objective, but they are a goal in themselves. Chat rooms have been around since the early days of the internet, but the virtual explosion of members of Web Log sites, and gaming communities have increased dramatically over the last decade (**Prove it**). The popularity of blogs has risen so drastically since there first appearance that there are now over fifty million blogers around the world.[3] Pornography also continues to be a mainstay of the internet with over 12 percent of all websites in existence being pornography related.[4]

---

[3] http://www.blogherald.com/2005/04/14/number-of-blogs-now-exceeds-50-million-worldwide/

[4] http://internet-filter-review.toptenreviews.com/internet-pornography-statistics.html#anchor4

(again you need to convince the reader that the online pornographer belongs with the blogger and the gamer...and how they are constantly connected.

Regardless of the number of opportunities provided to us by the internet, not all will find the same amount of use for it. Most have come to regard the internet as a tool to be utilized out of necessity, or in some cases convenience, while others have come to regard it as a unique experience in itself. Members of each of the three groups will agree, however, that the internet, like all tools, is meant to be exploited and taken advantage of for whatever means seem most appealing.

STEP TWO FROM WRITING MODULE THREE - CAUSE/EFFECT ESSAYS

FUN COMPREHENSION QUIZ

Below is a multiple choice quiz for you to do to check your understanding of the movie on a fairly simple level. It is difficult to analyze something when you don't have the basics; the movie is the basics, so do the quiz and use it to clarify points in the story about which you might be be sure.

Groundhog Day– Part One

1. At the beginning of the movie, they show Phil Connors doing the weather. What is the initial impression the movie gives us of the workplace?

    a.It's boring
    b.It's competitive
    c.It's unfair
    d.It's analytical

2. The opening scene shows Phil to be
    a. smart
    b. sarcastic
    c. bored
    d. all of the above

3. How many times in total (including this one) has Phil covered the Groundhog celebration?
    a. Two times
    b. Three times
    c. Four times
    d. Five times

4. I am the cameraman at Channel 9 Pittsburgh who also drives the news van.
    a. Barry
    b. Larry

c. Ned
d. Phil
5. I am the newly-hired producer of Channel 9 Pittsburgh. I am also a sucker for French poetry and rhinestones.
   a. Sara
   b. Rita
   c. Susan
   d. Nancy

6. What does Rita think of the groundhog?
   a. she thinks it's cute
   b. she thinks its rude
   c. she thinks it's disgusting
   d. she thinks it tastes good

7. What time does Phil wake up on Groundhog Day?
   a. 5:00
   b. 6:00
   c. 7:00
   d. 8:00

8. Why does Phil think that Ned is talking to him?
   a. he is an old friend
   b. he saw him on TV and wants to say hi
   c. he wants to sell him insurance
   d. he wants to see his sister again

9. In Ned and Phil's interaction, we see Ned to be what kind of person?
   a. Kind and caring
   b. Sad and lonely
   c. Selfless and funny
   d. Awkward and needy

10. Who worked in a Punxsatawney dress shop and went to Lincoln High School?
    a. Sara
    b. Nancy
    c. Rita
    d. Susan

11. I am a sweet grandmotherly-type lady who runs a very nice bed and breakfast on Cherry Street in Punxsatawny, PA. What is my name?
    a. Mrs. Lincoln
    b. Mrs. Lancaster
    c. Mrs. Leicester
    d. Mrs. Smith

12. I am the homeless man whom Phil Connors tries to prevent from dying on Groundhog Day. Although my name is never mentioned, what does Phil refer to me as?
    a. Dirty
    b. Pops
    c. Dad
    d. Bill

13. Phil breaks a pencil in half and puts it in front of the clock. What has happened to the pencil when he wakes up?
    a. it is still broken in half
    b. it has disappeared
    c. it is whole again
    d. what pencil?

14. When Phil is in the bowling alley, he talks with two guys. In the conversation there and in the car, Phil makes the realization that:
    a. he's a glass half-empty kind of guy
    b. he can't let people drive drunk
    c. he doesn't live by the rules anymore

15. One morning when Phil wakes up, he's happy; he kisses Mrs. Lancaster, punches Ned, lets someone else fall in the puddle. Why?
    a. he realizes there are no consequences
    b. he has accepted his situation and is happy
    c. he is an egomaniac and nothing will change that
    d. he really hates Ned and other people

16. Phil Connors must live the same day over and over again, and is forced to realize that the only real change that will ever be possible must happen _____
   a. within himself
   b. slowly
   c. with other people
   d. in the future

17. Over the course of the movie, Phil does not learn what:
   a. to play piano
   b. to ice sculpt
   c. to read Italian poetry
   d. to save people

18. Phil is a weatherman; the writer chose this profession probably because:
   a. weathermen always think they are more important than other people
   b. the blizzard was necessary to move the plot along
   c. weather is constantly changing but still remains the same
   d. weathermen are funny

19. When Phil begins to realize the power of repeating the same day he does which of the following:
   a. seduces Nancy
   b. steals money
   c. treats people with disrespect
   d. all of the above

20. Phil sets his sights on seducing Rita in the same way he seduced other women. Why does Phil need to seduce Rita?
   a. He is bored
   b. He thinks he loves her
   c. She is the ultimate challenge for him
   d. He is afraid that she will tell others that he is reliving the same day

21. Finally, Phil gets Rita to his room but Rita still rejects him. Why?
   a. she doesn't really like him
   b. she senses he is trying to manipulate her
   c. she wants him to tell her he loves her
   d. she doesn't like the fudge she ate

22. After the above rejection, we see the repeats of the day. How does each one end?
    a. with Phil walking past the ice sculptures
    b. with Phil taking a shower
    c. with Phil more determined than ever
    d. with Phil being rejected

23. On one of the Groundhog Day changes, the clock changes slowly and there is no song in the morning. Why do you think this is?
    a. to keep the audience interested
    b. to signify a change in Phil
    c. to show that time is about to change

24. After the slow clock change, Phil becomes:
    a. more arrogant
    b. more optimistic
    c. more outgoing
    d. more depressed

25. Why does Phil decide to steal the groundhog?
    a. he believes he can do whatever he wants and it doesn't matter
    b. he believes that the groundhog is ugly
    c. he believes that the groundhog is inextricably tied to his current predicament
    d. he acts on impulse without thinking

26. Phil steals the groundhog and a car chase ensues. What happens at the end of the car chase?
    a. the police arrest Phil
    b. Rita cries
    c. Phil throws the groundhog out of the window
    d. Phil drives himself off the cliff

27. Which of the following do we not see Phil try:
    a. electrocution
    b. poisoning
    c. jumping from a tall building
    d. crashing a car

28. After dying over and over, Phil comes to the understanding that he is:
    a. worthy of great things
    b. godlike
    c. doomed forever
    d. crazy

29. At the end of his tether, Phil makes Rita believe what is happening by:
    a. standing in front of a truck and killing himself
    b. killing the groundhog
    c. predicting the whole day's events
    d. telling her about everyone in the diner

30. Rita puts forth another way of perceiving the day:
    a. it's fun
    b. it's not a curse
    c. it's not an opportunity to be a god

31. Who is the first person the changed Phil becomes really invested in?
    a. Ned
    b. Nancy
    c. Pops
    d. Hall guy

32. Changed Phil begins to learn the piano and to ice sculpt. Why?
    a. he is bored
    b. it is the only way to make Rita love him
    c. it brings him praise
    d. he wants to

33. Who says, "sometimes, I wish I had a thousand lifetimes"?
    a. Phil
    b. Rita
    c. Larry
    d. Pops

34. Why is Phil so invested in keeping the homeless man alive?
   a. he believes that he can save him
   b. he loves him
   c. he needs to feel in control of something
   d. Rita won't love him if he dies

35. Given that the homeless guy does die. What can Phil do for him?
   a. Nothing at all
   b. Find him a good doctor
   c. Not let him die in the street
   d. Give him money

36. When Phil arrives at Gobbler's knob one morning, how do we know something is different?
   a. He is carrying coffee
   b. He asks Larry his opinion
   c. He is interested in his report
   d. All of the above

37. Which famous writer does Phil quote in his groundhog report on his final groundhog day?
   a. Sir Walter Scott
   b. Baudelaire
   c. Shakespeare
   d. Chekhov

38. Which of the following "errands" does fill not run on the final Groundhog Day?
   a. fixing a flat tire
   b. performing the Heimlich maneuver
   c. having dinner with Rita
   d. shouting at the kid who falls from the tree
   e. playing at the Groundhog Dinner

39. Phil learns that if he does not contribute to the people around him:
   a. tomorrow will not be Groundhog Day
   b. his abilities will disappear
   c. those people will suffer in some way
   d. Rita will leave him

40. Which of the following lessons does Phil learn throughout the movie:
   a. fame is more important than friendship
   b. life without consequences is the best way to live
   c. his terrible childhood led him to this point
   d. a disinterest in self indirectly promotes happiness within

Who said it?
Identify the source of each quotation. The name choices are the same for each one.
   a. Phil   b. Rita   c. Larry   d. Nancy   e.Ned

   41. "Maybe it's not a curse."
   42. "People are morons."
   43. Did he actually call himself the talent?"
   44. "I don't even like myself."
   45. You couldn't plan a day like this."
   46. "When I see an opportunity, I charge it like a bull."
   47. "I've come to the end of me."
   48. "What if there is no tomorrow; there wasn't one today."
   49. "You love me? You don't even know me."
   50. "I just like to go with the flow."

Quiz Part B
   1. List two adjectives that describe Phil's character before he changes. Provide specific
   support to justify your choice of each adjective.
a.

b.

   2. List two adjectives that describe Phil's character after he changes. Provide specific
   support to justify your choice of each adjective.
a.

b.

APPENDIX E
Short Stories

Story 1 Araby by James Joyce

NORTH RICHMOND STREET being blind, was a quiet street except at the hour when the Christian Brothers' School set the boys free. An uninhabited house of two storeys stood at the blind end, detached from its neighbours in a square ground The other houses of the street, conscious of decent lives within them, gazed at one another with brown imperturbable faces

The former tenant of our house, a priest, had died in the back drawing-room. Air, musty from having been long enclosed, hung in all the rooms, and the waste room behind the kitchen was littered with old useless papers. Among these I found a few paper-covered books, the pages of which were curled and damp: The Abbot, by Walter Scott, The Devout Communnicant and The Memoirs of Vidocq. I liked the last best because its leaves were yellow. The wild garden behind the house contained a central apple-tree and a few straggling bushes under one of which I found the late tenant's rusty bicycle-pump. He had been a very charitable priest; in his will he had left all his money to institutions and the furniture of his house to his sister.

When the short days of winter came dusk fell before we had well eaten our dinners. When we met in the street the houses had grown sombre. The space of sky above us was the colour of ever-changing violet and towards it the lamps of the street lifted their feeble lanterns. The cold air stung us and we played till our bodies glowed. Our shouts echoed in the silent street. The career of our play brought us through the dark muddy lanes behind the houses where we ran the gauntlet of the rough tribes from the cottages, to the back doors of the dark dripping gardens where odours arose from the ashpits, to the dark odorous stables where a coachman smoothed and combed the horse or shook music from the buckled harness. When we returned to the street light from the kitchen windows had filled the areas. If my uncle was seen turning the corner we hid in the shadow until we had seen him safely housed. Or if Mangan's sister came out on the doorstep to call her brother in to his tea we watched her from our shadow peer up and down the street. We waited to see whether she would remain or go in and, if she remained, we left our shadow and walked up to Mangan's steps resignedly. She was waiting for us, her figure defined by the light from the half-opened door. Her brother always teased her before he obeyed and I stood by the railings looking at her. Her dress swung as she moved her body and the soft rope of her hair tossed from side to side.

Every morning I lay on the floor in the front parlour watching her door. The blind was pulled down to within an inch of the sash so that I could not be seen. When she came out on the doorstep my heart leaped. I ran to the hall, seized my books and followed her. I kept her brown figure always in my eye and, when we came near the point at which our ways diverged, I quickened my pace and passed her. This happened morning after morning. I had never spoken to her, except for a few casual words, and yet her name was like a summons to all my foolish blood.

Her image accompanied me even in places the most hostile to romance. On Saturday evenings when my aunt went marketing I had to go to carry some of the parcels. We walked through the flaring streets, jostled by drunken men and bargaining women, amid the curses of labourers, the shrill litanies of shop-boys who stood on guard by the barrels of pigs' cheeks, the nasal chanting of street-singers, who sang a come-all-you about O'Donovan Rossa, or a ballad about the troubles in our native land. These noises converged in a single sensation of life for me: I imagined that I bore my chalice safely through a throng of foes. Her name sprang to my lips at moments in strange prayers and praises which I myself did not understand. My eyes were often full of tears (I could not tell why) and at times a flood from my heart seemed to pour itself out into my bosom. I thought little of the future. I did not know whether I would ever speak to her or not or, if I spoke to her, how I could tell her of my confused adoration. But my body was like a harp and her words and gestures were like fingers running upon the wires.

One evening I went into the back drawing-room in which the priest had died. It was a dark rainy evening and there was no sound in the house. Through one of the broken panes I heard the rain impinge upon the earth, the fine incessant needles of water playing in the sodden beds. Some distant lamp or lighted window gleamed below me. I was thankful that I could see so little. All my senses seemed to desire to veil themselves and, feeling that I was about to slip from them, I pressed the palms of my hands together until they trembled, murmuring: "O love! O love!" many times.

At last she spoke to me. When she addressed the first words to me I was so confused that I did not know what to answer. She asked me was I going to Araby. I forgot whether I answered yes or no. It would be a splendid bazaar, she said she would love to go.

213

"And why can't you?" I asked.

While she spoke she turned a silver bracelet round and round her wrist. She could not go, she said, because there would be a retreat that week in her convent. Her brother and two other boys were fighting for their caps and I was alone at the railings. She held one of the spikes, bowing her head towards me. The light from the lamp opposite our door caught the white curve of her neck, lit up her hair that rested there and, falling, lit up the hand upon the railing. It fell over one side of her dress and caught the white border of a petticoat, just visible as she stood at ease.

"It's well for you," she said.

"If I go," I said, "I will bring you something."

What innumerable follies laid waste my waking and sleeping thoughts after that evening! I wished to annihilate the tedious intervening days. I chafed against the work of school. At night in my bedroom and by day in the classroom her image came between me and the page I strove to read. The syllables of the word Araby were called to me through the silence in which my soul luxuriated and cast an Eastern enchantment over me. I asked for leave to go to the bazaar on Saturday night. My aunt was surprised and hoped it was not some Freemason affair. I answered few questions in class. I watched my master's face pass from amiability to sternness; he hoped I was not beginning to idle. I could not call my wandering thoughts together. I had hardly any patience with the serious work of life which, now that it stood between me and my desire, seemed to me child's play, ugly monotonous child's play.

On Saturday morning I reminded my uncle that I wished to go to the bazaar in the evening. He was fussing at the hallstand, looking for the hat-brush, and answered me curtly:

"Yes, boy, I know."

As he was in the hall I could not go into the front parlour and lie at the window. I left the house in bad humour and walked slowly towards the school. The air was pitilessly raw and already my heart misgave me.

When I came home to dinner my uncle had not yet been home. Still it was early. I sat staring at the clock for some time and. when its ticking began to irritate me, I left the room. I mounted the staircase and gained the upper part of the house. The high cold empty gloomy rooms liberated me and I went from room to room singing. From the front window I saw my companions playing below in the street. Their cries reached me weakened and indistinct and, leaning my forehead against the cool glass, I looked over at the dark house where she lived. I may have stood there for an hour, seeing nothing but the brown-clad figure cast by my imagination, touched discreetly by the lamplight at the curved neck, at the hand upon the railngs and at the border below the dress.

When I came downstairs again I found Mrs. Mercer sitting at the fire. She was an old garrulous woman, a pawnbroker's widow, who collected used stamps for some pious purpose. I had to endure the gossip of the tea-table. The meal was prolonged beyond an hour and still my uncle did not come. Mrs. Mercer stood up to go: she was sorry she couldn't wait any longer, but it was after eight o'clock and she did not like to be out late as the night air was bad for her. When she had gone I began to walk up and down the room, clenching my fists. My aunt said:

"I'm afraid you may put off your bazaar for this night of Our Lord."

At nine o'clock I heard my uncle's latchkey in the halldoor. I heard him talking to himself and heard the hallstand rocking when it had received the weight of his overcoat. I could interpret these signs. When he was midway through his dinner I asked him to give me the money to go to the bazaar. He had forgotten.

"The people are in bed and after their first sleepnow," he said.

I did not smile. My aunt said to him energetically:

"Can't you give him the money and let him go? You've kept him late enough as it is."

My uncle said he was very sorry he had forgotten. He said he believed in the old saying: "All work and no play makes Jack a dull boy." He asked me where I was going and, when I had told him a second time he asked me did I know The Arab's Farewell to his Steed. When I left the kitchen he was about to recite the opening lines of the piece to my aunt.

I held a florin tightly in my hand as I strode down Buckingham Street towards the station. The sight of the streets thronged with buyers and glaring with gas recalled to me the purpose of my journey. I took my seat in a third-class carriage of a deserted train. After an intolerable delay the train moved out of the station slowly. It crept onward among ruinous house and over the twinkling river. At Westland Row Station a crowd of people pressed to the carriage doors; but the porters moved them back, saying that it was a special train for the bazaar. I remained alone in the bare carriage. In a few minutes the train drew up beside an improvised wooden platform. I passed out on to the road and saw by the lighted dial of a clock that it was ten minutes to ten. In front of me was a large building which displayed the magical name.

I could not find any sixpenny entrance and, fearing that the bazaar would be closed, I passed in quickly through a turnstile, handing a shilling to a weary-looking man. I found myself in a big hall girdled at half its height by a gallery. Nearly all the stalls were closed and the greater part of the hall was in darkness. I recognised a silence like that which pervades a church after a service. I walked into the centre of the bazaar timidly. A few people were gathered about the stalls which were still open. Before a curtain, over which the words Cafe Chantant were written in coloured lamps, two men were counting money on a salver. I listened to the fall of the coins.

Remembering with difficulty why I had come I went over to one of the stalls and examined porcelain vases and flowered tea- sets. At the door of the stall a young lady was talking and laughing with two young gentlemen. I remarked their English accents and listened vaguely to their conversation.

"O, I never said such a thing!"

"O, but you did!"

"O, but I didn't!"

"Didn't she say that?"

"Yes. I heard her."

"0, there's a ... fib!"

Observing me the young lady came over and asked me did I wish to buy anything. The tone of her voice was not encouraging; she seemed to have spoken to me out of a sense of duty. I looked humbly at the great jars that stood like eastern guards at either side of the dark entrance to the stall and murmured:

"No, thank you."

The young lady changed the position of one of the vases and wentback to the two young men. They began to talk of the same subject. Once or twice the young lady glanced at me over her shoulder.

I lingered before her stall, though I knew my stay was useless, to make my interest in her wares seem the more real. Then I turned away slowly and walked down the middle of the bazaar. I allowed the two pennies to fall against the sixpence in my pocket. I heard a voice call from one end of the gallery that the light was out. The upper part of the hall was now completely dark.

Gazing up into the darkness I saw myself as a creature driven and derided by vanity; and my eyes burned with anguish and anger.

STORY 2 The Lottery by Shirley Jackson

THE MORNING of June 27th was clear and sunny, with the fresh warmth of a full-summer day; the flowers were blossoming profusely and the grass was richly green. The people of the village began to gather in the square, between the post office and the bank, around ten o'clock; in some towns there were so many people that the **lottery** took two days and had to be started on June 26th, but in this village, where there were only about three hundred people, the whole **lottery** took less than two hours, so it could begin at ten o'clock in the morning and still be through in time to allow the villagers to get home for noon dinner.

The children assembled first, of course. School was recently over for the summer, and the feeling of liberty sat uneasily on most of them; they tended to gather together quietly for a while before they broke into boisterous play, and their talk was still of the classroom and the teacher, of books and reprimands. Bobby Martin had already stuffed his pockets full of stones, and the other boys soon followed his example, selecting the smoothest and roundest stones; Bobby and Harry Jones and Dickie Delacroix -- the villagers pronounced this name "Dellacroy" -- eventually made a great pile of stones in one corner of the square and guarded it against the raids of the other boys. The girls stood aside, talking among themselves, looking over their shoulders at the boys, and the very small children rolled in the dust or clung to the hands of their older brothers or sisters.

Soon the men began to gather, surveying their own children, speaking of planting and rain, tractors and taxes. They stood together, away from the pile of stones in the corner, and their jokes were quiet and they smiled rather than laughed. The women, wearing faded housedresses and sweaters, came shortly after their men-folk. They greeted one another and exchanged bits of gossip as they went to join their husbands. Soon the women, standing by their husbands, began to call to their children, and the children came reluctantly, having to be called four or five times. Bobby Martin ducked under his mother's grasping hand and ran, laughing, back to the pile of stones. His father spoke up sharply, and Bobby came quickly and took his place between his father and his oldest brother.

The **lottery** was conducted -- as were the square dances, the teenage club, the Halloween program -- by Mr. Summers, who had time and energy to devote to civic activities. He was a round-faced, jovial man and he ran the coal business, and people were sorry for him, because he had no children and his wife was a scold. When he arrived in the square, carrying the black wooden box, there was a murmur of conversation among the villagers, and he waved and called, "Little late today, folks." The postmaster, Mr. Graves, followed him, carrying a three-legged stool, and the stool was put in the center of the square and Mr. Summers set the black box down on it. The villagers kept their distance, leaving a space between themselves and the stool, and when Mr. Summers said, "Some of you fellows want to give me a hand?" there was a hesitation before two men, Mr. Martin and his oldest son, Baxter, came forward to hold the box steady on the stool while Mr. Summers stirred up the papers inside it.

The original paraphernalia for the **lottery** had been lost long ago, and the black box now resting on the stool had been put into use even before Old Man Warner, the oldest man in town, was born. Mr. Summers spoke frequently to the villagers about making a new box, but no one liked to upset even as much tradition as was represented by the black box. There was a story that the present box had been made with some pieces of the box that had preceded it, the one that had been constructed when the first people settled down to make a village here. Every year, after the **lottery**, Mr. Summers began talking again about a new box, but every year the subject was allowed to fade off without anything's being done. The black box grew shabbier each year; by now it was no longer completely black but splintered badly along one side to show the original wood color, and in some places faded or stained.

Mr. Martin and his oldest son, Baxter, held the black box securely on the stool until Mr. Summers had stirred the papers thoroughly with his hand. Because so much of the ritual had been forgotten or discarded, Mr. Summers had been successful in having slips of paper substituted for the chips of wood that had been used for generations. Chips of wood, Mr. Summers had argued, had been all very well when the village was tiny, but now that the population was more than three hundred and likely to keep on growing, it was necessary to use something that would fit more easily into the black box. The night before the **lottery**, Mr. Summers and Mr. Graves made up the slips of paper and put them in the box, and it was then taken to the safe of Mr. Summers's coal company and locked up until Mr. Summers was ready to take it to the square next morning. The rest of the year, the box was put away, sometimes one place, sometimes another; it had spent one year in Mr. Graves's barn and another year underfoot in the post office, and sometimes it was set on a shelf in the Martin grocery and left there.

There was a great deal of fussing to be done before Mr. Summers declared the **lottery** open. There were the lists to make up -- of heads of families, heads of households in each family, members of each household in each family. There was the proper swearing-in of Mr. Summers by the postmaster, as the official of the**lottery**; at one time, some people remembered, there had been a recital of some sort, performed by the official of the **lottery**, a perfunctory, tuneless chant that had been rattled off duly each year; some people believed

that the official of the **lottery** used to stand just so when he said or sang it, others believed that he was supposed to walk among the people, but years and years ago this part of the ritual had been allowed to lapse. There had been, also, a ritual salute, which the official of the **lottery** had had to use in addressing each person who came up to draw from the box, but this also had changed with time, until now it was felt necessary only for the official to speak to each person approaching. Mr. Summers was very good at all this; in his clean white shirt and blue jeans, with one hand resting carelessly on the black box, he seemed very proper and important as he talked interminably to Mr. Graves and the Martins.

Just as Mr. Summers finally left off talking and turned to the assembled villagers, Mrs. Hutchinson came hurriedly along the path to the square, her sweater thrown over her shoulders, and slid into place in the back of the crowd. "Clean forgot what day it was," she said to Mrs. Delacroix, who stood next to her, and they both laughed softly. "Thought my old man was out back stacking wood," Mrs. Hutchinson went on, "and then I looked out the window and the kids was gone, and then I remembered it was the twenty-seventh and came a-running." She dried her hands on her apron, and Mrs. Delacroix said, "You're in time, though. They're still talking away up there."

Mrs. Hutchinson craned her neck to see through the crowd and found her husband and children standing near the front. She tapped Mrs. Delacroix on the arm as a farewell and began to make her way through the crowd. The people separated good-humoredly to let her through; two or three people said, in voices just loud enough to be heard across the crowd, "Here comes your Missus, Hutchinson," and "Bill, she made it after all." Mrs. Hutchinson reached her husband, and Mr. Summers, who had been waiting, said cheerfully, "Thought we were going to have to get on without you, Tessie." Mrs. Hutchinson said, grinning, "Wouldn't have me leave m'dishes in the sink, now, would you, Joe?" and soft laughter ran through the crowd as the people stirred back into position after Mrs. Hutchinson's arrival.

"Well, now," Mr. Summers said soberly, "guess we better get started, get this over with, so's we can go back to work. Anybody ain't here?"

"Dunbar," several people said. "Dunbar, Dunbar."

Mr. Summers consulted his list. "Clyde Dunbar," he said. "That's right. He's broke his leg, hasn't he? Who's drawing for him?"

"Me, I guess," a woman said, and Mr. Summers turned to look at her. "Wife draws for her husband," Mr. Summers said. "Don't you have a grown boy to do it for you, Janey?" Although Mr. Summers and everyone else in the village knew the answer perfectly well, it was the business of the official of the **lottery** to ask such questions formally. Mr. Summers waited with an expression of polite interest while Mrs. Dunbar answered.

"Horace's not but sixteen yet," Mrs. Dunbar said regretfully. "Guess I gotta fill in for the old man this year."

"Right," Mr. Summers said. He made a note on the list he was holding. Then he asked, "Watson boy drawing this year?"

A tall boy in the crowd raised his hand. "Here," he said. "I'm drawing for m'mother and me." He blinked his eyes nervously and ducked his head as several voices in the crowd said things like "Good fellow, Jack," and "Glad to see your mother's got a man to do it."

"Well," Mr. Summers said, "guess that's everyone. Old Man Warner make it?"

"Here," a voice said, and Mr. Summers nodded.

A sudden hush fell on the crowd as Mr. Summers cleared his throat and looked at the list. "All ready?" he called. "Now, I'll read the names -- heads of families first -- and the men come up and take a paper out of the box. Keep the paper folded in your hand without looking at it until everyone has had a turn. Everything clear?"

The people had done it so many times that they only half listened to the directions; most of them were quiet, wetting their lips, not looking around. Then Mr. Summers raised one hand high and said, "Adams." A man disengaged himself from the crowd and came forward. "Hi, Steve," Mr. Summers said, and Mr. Adams said, "Hi, Joe." They grinned at one another humorlessly and nervously. Then Mr. Adams reached into the black box and took out a folded paper. He held it firmly by one corner as he turned and went hastily back to his place in the crowd, where he stood a little apart from his family, not looking down at his hand.

"Allen," Mr. Summers said. "Anderson .... Bentham."

"Seems like there's no time at all between lotteries anymore," Mrs. Delacroix said to Mrs. Graves in the back row. "Seems like we got through with the last one only last week."

"Time sure goes fast," Mrs. Graves said.

"Clark.... Delacroix."

"There goes my old man," Mrs. Delacroix said. She held her breath while her husband went forward.

"Dunbar," Mr. Summers said, and Mrs. Dunbar went steadily to the box while one of the women said, "Go on, Janey," and another said, "There she goes."

"We're next," Mrs. Graves said. She watched while Mr. Graves came around from the side of the box, greeted Mr. Summers gravely, and selected a slip of paper from the box. By now, all through the crowd there were men holding the small folded papers in their large hands, turning them over and over nervously. Mrs. Dunbar and her two sons stood together, Mrs. Dunbar holding the slip of paper.

"Harburt .... Hutchinson."

"Get up there, Bill," Mrs. Hutchinson said, and the people near her laughed.

"Jones."

"They do say," Mr. Adams said to Old Man Warner, who stood next to him, "that over in the north village they're talking of giving up the **lottery**."
Old Man Warner snorted. "Pack of crazy fools," he said. "Listening to the young folks, nothing's good enough for *them*. Next thing you know, they'll be wanting to go back to living in caves, nobody work anymore, live *that* way for a while. Used to be a saying about 'Lottery in June, corn be heavy soon.' First thing you know, we'd all be eating stewed chickweed and acorns. There's *always* been a **lottery**," he added petulantly. "Bad enough to see young Joe Summers up there joking with everybody."

"Some places have already quit lotteries," Mrs. Adams said.

"Nothing but trouble in *that*," Old Man Warner said stoutly. "Pack of young fools."

"Martin." And Bobby Martin watched his father go forward. "Overdyke .... Percy."

"I wish they'd hurry," Mrs. Dunbar said to her older son. "I wish they'd hurry."

"They're almost through," her son said.

"You get ready to run tell Dad," Mrs. Dunbar said.

Mr. Summers called his own name and then stepped forward precisely and selected a slip from the box. Then he called, "Warner."

"Seventy-seventh year I been in the **lottery**," Old Man Warner said as he went through the crowd. "Seventy-seventh time."

"Watson." The tall boy came awkwardly through the crowd. Someone said, "Don't be nervous, Jack," and Mr. Summers said, "Take your time, son."

"Zanini."

After that, there was a long pause, a breathless pause, until Mr. Summers, holding his slip of paper in the air, said, "All right, fellows." For a minute, no one moved, and then all the slips of paper were opened. Suddenly, all the women began to speak at once, saying, "Who is it?" "Who's got it?" "Is it the Dunbars?" "Is it the Watsons?" Then the voices began to say, "It's Hutchinson. It's Bill." "Bill Hutchinson's got it." "Go tell your father," Mrs. Dunbar said to her older son. People began to look around to see the Hutchinsons. Bill Hutchinson was standing quiet, staring down at the paper in his hand. Suddenly, Tessie Hutchinson shouted to Mr. Summers. "You didn't give him time enough to take any paper he wanted. I saw you. It wasn't fair!"

"Be a good sport, Tessie," Mrs. Delacroix called, and Mrs. Graves said, "All of us took the same chance."

"Shut up, Tessie," Bill Hutchinson said.

"Well, everyone," Mr. Summers said, "that was done pretty fast, and now we've got to be hurrying a little more to get done in time." He consulted his next list. "Bill," he said, "you draw for the Hutchinson family. You got any other households in the Hutchinsons?"

"There's Don and Eva," Mrs. Hutchinson yelled. "Make *them* take their chance!"

"Daughters draw with their husbands' families, Tessie," Mr. Summers said gently. "You know that as well as anyone else."

"It wasn't *fair*," Tessie said.

"I guess not, Joe," Bill Hutchinson said regretfully. "My daughter draws with her husband's family, that's only fair. And I've got no other family except the kids."

"Then, as far as drawing for families is concerned, it's you," Mr. Summers said in explanation, "and as far as drawing for households is concerned, that's you, too. Right?"

"Right," Bill Hutchinson said.

"How many kids, Bill?" Mr. Summers asked formally.

"There," Bill Hutchinson said. "There's Bill, Jr., and Nancy, and little Dave. And Tessie and me."

"All right, then," Mr. Summers said. "Harry, you got their tickets back?"

Mr. Graves nodded and held up the slips of paper. "Put them in the box, then," Mr. Summers directed. "Take Bill's and put it in."

"I think we ought to start over," Mrs. Hutchinson said, as quietly as she could. "I tell you it wasn't fair. You didn't give him time enough to choose. Everybody saw that."

Mr. Graves had selected the five slips and put them in the box, and he dropped all the papers but those onto the ground, where the breeze caught them and lifted them off.

"Listen, everybody," Mrs. Hutchinson was saying to the people around her.

"Ready, Bill')" Mr. Summers asked, and Bill Hutchinson, with one quick glance around at his wife and children, nodded.

"Remember," Mr. Summers said, "take the slips and keep them folded until each person has taken one. Harry, you help little Dave." Mr. Graves took the hand of the little boy, who came willingly with him up to the box. "Take a paper out of the box, Davy," Mr. Summers said. Davy put his hand into the box and laughed. "Take just *one paper*," Mr. Summers said. "Harry, you hold it for him." Mr. Graves took the child's hand and removed the folded paper from the tight fist and held it while little Dave stood next to him and looked up at him wonderingly.

"Nancy next," Mr. Summers said. Nancy was twelve, and her school friends breathed heavily as she went forward, switching her skirt, and took a slip daintily from the box. "Bill, Jr.," Mr. Summers said, and Billy, his face red and his feet overlarge, nearly knocked the box over as he got a paper out. "Tessie," Mr. Summers said. She hesitated for a minute, looking around defiantly, and then set her lips and went up to the box. She snatched a paper out and held it behind her.

"Bill," Mr. Summers said, and Bill Hutchinson reached into the box and felt around, bringing his hand out at last with the slip of paper in it.

The crowd was quiet. A girt whispered, "I hope it's not Nancy," and the sound of the whisper reached the edges of the crowd.

"It's not the way it used to be," Old Man Warner said clearly. "People ain't the way they used to be."

"All right," Mr. Summers said. "Open the papers. Harry, you open little Dave's."

Mr. Graves opened the slip of paper and there was a general sigh through the crowd as he held it up and everyone could see that it was blank. Nancy and Bill, Jr., opened theirs at the same time, and both beamed and laughed, turning around to the crowd and holding their slips of paper above their heads.

"Tessie," Mr. Summers said. There was a pause, and then Mr. Summers looked at Bill Hutchinson, and Bill unfolded his paper and showed it. It was blank.

"It's Tessie," Mr. Summers said, and his voice was hushed. "Show us her paper, Bill."

Bill Hutchinson went over to his wife and forced the slip of paper out of her hand. It had a black spot on it, the black spot Mr. Summers had made the night before with the heavy pencil in the coalcompany office. Bill Hutchinson held it up, and there was a stir in the crowd.

"All right, folks," Mr. Summers said. "Let's finish quickly."

Although the villagers had forgotten the ritual and lost the original black box, they still remembered to use stones. The pile of stones the boys had made earlier was ready; there were stones on the ground with the blowing scraps of paper that had come out of the box. Mrs. Delacroix selected a stone so large she had to pick it up with both hands and turned to Mrs. Dunbar. "Come on," she said. "Hurry up."

Mrs. Dunbar had small stones in both hands, and she said, gasping for breath, "I can't run at all. You'll have to go ahead and I'll catch up with you."

The children had stones already and someone gave little Davy Hutchinson a few pebbles.

Tessie Hutchinson was in the center of a cleared space by now, and she held her hands out desperately as the villagers moved in on her. "It isn't fair," she said. A stone hit her on the side of the head.

Old Man Warner was saying, "Come on, come on, everyone."

Steve Adams was in the front of the crowd of villagers, with Mrs. Graves beside him.

"It isn't fair, it isn't right," Mrs. Hutchinson screamed, and then they were upon her.

STORY 3 A Rose for Emily by William Faulkner

When Miss Emily Grierson died, our whole town went to her funeral: the men through a sort of respectful affection for a fallen monument, the women mostly out of curiosity to see the inside of her house, which no one save an old man-servant—a combined gardener and cook—had seen in at least ten years.

It was a big, squarish frame house that had once been white, decorated with cupolas and spires and scrolled balconies in the heavily lightsome style of the seventies, set on what had once been our most select street. But garages and cotton gins had encroached and obliterated even the august names of that neighborhood; only Miss Emily's house was left, lifting its stubborn and coquettish decay above the cotton wagons and the gasoline pumps—an eyesore among eyesores. And now Miss Emily had gone to join the representatives of those august names where they lay in the cedar-bemused cemetery among the ranked and anonymous graves of Union and Confederate soldiers who fell at the battle of Jefferson.

Alive, Miss Emily had been a tradition, a duty, and a care; a sort of hereditary obligation upon the town, dating from that day in 1894 when Colonel Sartoris, the mayor—he who fathered the edict that no Negro woman should appear on the streets without an apron—remitted her taxes, the dispensation dating from the death of her father on into perpetuity. Not that Miss Emily would have accepted charity. Colonel Sartoris invented an involved tale to the effect that Miss Emily's father had loaned money to the town, which the town, as a matter of business, preferred this way of repaying. Only a man of Colonel Sartoris' generation and thought could have invented it, and only a woman could have believed it.

When the next generation, with its more modern ideas, became mayors and aldermen, this arrangement created some little dissatisfaction. On the first of the year they mailed her a tax notice. February came, and there was no reply. They wrote her a formal letter, asking her to call at the sheriff's office at her convenience. A week later the mayor wrote her himself, offering to call or to send his car for her, and received in reply a note on paper of an archaic shape, in a thin, flowing calligraphy in faded ink, to the effect that she no longer went out at all. The tax notice was also enclosed, without comment.

They called a special meeting of the Board of Aldermen. A deputation waited upon her, knocked at the door through which no visitor had passed since she ceased giving china-painting lessons eight or ten years earlier. They were admitted by the old Negro into a dim hall from which a stairway mounted into still more shadow. It smelled of dust and disuse—a close, dank smell. The Negro led them into the parlor. It was furnished in heavy, leather-covered furniture. When the Negro opened the blinds of one window, they could see that the leather was cracked; and when they sat down, a faint dust rose sluggishly about their thighs, spinning with slow motes in the single sun-ray. On a tarnished gilt easel before the fireplace stood a crayon portrait of Miss Emily's father.

They rose when she entered—a small, fat woman in black, with a thin gold chain descending to her waist and vanishing into her belt, leaning on an ebony cane with a tarnished gold head. Her skeleton was small and spare; perhaps that was why what would have been merely plumpness in another was obesity in her. She looked bloated, like a body long submerged in motionless water, and of that pallid hue. Her eyes, lost in the fatty ridges of her face, looked like two small pieces of coal pressed into a lump of dough as they moved from one face to another while the visitors stated their errand.

She did not ask them to sit. She just stood in the door and listened quietly until the spokesman came to a stumbling halt. Then they could hear the invisible watch ticking at the end of the gold chain.

Her voice was dry and cold. "I have no taxes in Jefferson. Colonel Sartoris explained it to me. Perhaps one of you can gain access to the city records and satisfy yourselves."

"But we have. We are the city authorities, Miss Emily. Didn't you get a notice from the sheriff, signed by him?"

"I received a paper, yes," Miss Emily said. "Perhaps he considers himself the sheriff . . . I have no taxes in Jefferson."

"But there is nothing on the books to show that, you see. We must go by the—"

"See Colonel Sartoris. I have no taxes in Jefferson."

"But, Miss Emily—"

"See Colonel Sartoris." (Colonel Sartoris had been dead almost ten years.) "I have no taxes in Jefferson. Tobe!" The Negro appeared. "Show these gentlemen out."

So she vanquished them, horse and foot, just as she had vanquished their fathers thirty years before about the smell. That was two years after her father's death and a short time after her sweetheart—the one we believed would marry her—had deserted her. After her father's death she went out very little; after her sweetheart went away, people hardly saw her at all. A few of the ladies had the temerity to call, but were not received, and the only sign of life about the place was the Negro man—a young man then—going in and out with a market basket.

"Just as if a man—any man—could keep a kitchen properly," the ladies said; so they were not surprised when the smell developed. It was another link between the gross, teeming world and the high and mighty Griersons.

A neighbor, a woman, complained to the mayor, Judge Stevens, eighty years old.

"But what will you have me do about it, madam?" he said.

"Why, send her word to stop it," the woman said. "Isn't there a law?"

"I'm sure that won't be necessary," Judge Stevens said. "It's probably just a snake or a rat that nigger of hers killed in the yard. I'll speak to him about it."

The next day he received two more complaints, one from a man who came in diffident deprecation. "We really must do something about it, Judge. I'd be the last one in the world to bother Miss Emily, but we've got to do something." That night the Board of Aldermen met--three graybeards and one younger man, a member of the rising generation.

"It's simple enough," he said. "Send her word to have her place cleaned up. Give her a certain time to do it in, and if she don't . . ."

"Dammit, sir," Judge Stevens said, "will you accuse a lady to her face of smelling bad?"

So the next night, after midnight, four men crossed Miss Emily's lawn and slunk about the house like burglars, sniffing along the base of the brickwork and at the cellar openings while one of them performed a regular sowing motion with his hand out of a sack slung from his shoulder. They broke open the cellar door and sprinkled lime there, and in all the outbuildings. As they recrossed the lawn, a window that had been dark was lighted and Miss Emily sat in it, the light behind her, and her upright torso motionless as that of an idol. They crept quietly across the lawn and into the shadow of the locusts that lined the street. After a week or two the smell went away.

That was when people had begun to feel really sorry for her. People in our town, remembering how old lady Wyatt, her great-aunt, had gone completely crazy at last, believed that the Griersons held themselves a little too high for what they really were. None of the young men were quite good enough for Miss Emily and such. We had long thought of them as a tableau, Miss Emily a slender figure in white in the background, her father a spraddled silhouette in the foreground, his back to her and clutching a horsewhip, the two of them framed by the back-flung front door. So when she got to be thirty and was still single, we were not pleased exactly, but vindicated; even with insanity in the family she wouldn't have turned down all of her chances if they had really materialized.

When her father died, it got about that the house was all that was left to her; and in a way, people were glad. At last they could pity Miss Emily. Being left alone, and a pauper, she had become humanized. Now she too would know the old thrill and the old despair of a penny more or less.

The day after his death all the ladies prepared to call at the house and offer condolence and aid, as is our custom Miss Emily met them at the door, dressed as usual and with no trace of grief on her face. She told them that her father was not dead. She did that for three days, with the ministers calling on her, and the doctors, trying to persuade her to let them dispose of the body. Just as they were about to resort to law and force, she broke down, and they buried her father quickly.

We did not say she was crazy then. We believed she had to do that. We remembered all the young men her father had driven away, and we knew that with nothing left, she would have to cling to that which had robbed her, as people will.

She was sick for a long time. When we saw her again, her hair was cut short, making her look like a girl, with a vague resemblance to those angels in colored church windows—sort of tragic and serene.

The town had just let the contracts for paving the sidewalks, and in the summer after her father's death they began the work. The construction company came with riggers and mules and machinery, and a foreman named Homer Barron, a Yankee—a big, dark, ready man, with a big voice and eyes lighter than his face. The little boys would follow in groups to hear him cuss the riggers, and the riggers singing in time to the rise and fall of picks. Pretty soon he knew everybody in town. Whenever you heard a lot of laughing anywhere about the square, Homer Barron would be in the center of the group. Presently we began to see him and Miss Emily on Sunday afternoons driving in the yellow-wheeled buggy and the matched team of bays from the livery stable.

At first we were glad that Miss Emily would have an interest, because the ladies all said, "Of course a Grierson would not think seriously of a Northerner, a day laborer." But there were still others, older people, who said that even grief could not cause a real lady to forget noblesse oblige—without calling it noblesse oblige. They just said, "Poor Emily. Her kinsfolk should come to her." She had some kin in Alabama; but years ago her father had fallen out with them over the estate of old lady Wyatt, the crazy woman, and there was no communication between the two families. They had not even been represented at the funeral.

And as soon as the old people said, "Poor Emily," the whispering began. "Do you suppose it's really so?" they said to one another. "Of course it is. What else could . . ." This behind their hands; rustling of craned silk and satin behind jalousies closed upon the sun of Sunday afternoon as the thin, swift clop-clop-clop of the matched team passed: "Poor Emily."

She carried her head high enough—even when we believed that she was fallen. It was as if she demanded more than ever the recognition of her dignity as the last Grierson; as if it had wanted that touch of earthiness to reaffirm her imperviousness. Like when she bought the rat poison, the arsenic. That was over a year after they had begun to say "Poor Emily," and while the two female cousins were visiting her.

"I want some poison," she said to the druggist. She was over thirty then, still a slight woman, though thinner than usual, with cold, haughty black eyes in a face the flesh of which was strained across the temples and about the eye-sockets as you imagine a lighthouse-keeper's face ought to look. "I want some poison," she said.

"Yes, Miss Emily. What kind? For rats and such? I'd recom—"

"I want the best you have. I don't care what kind."

The druggist named several. "They'll kill anything up to an elephant. But what you want is—"

"Arsenic," Miss Emily said. "Is that a good one?"

"Is . . . arsenic? Yes, ma'am. But what you want—"

"I want arsenic."

The druggist looked down at her. She looked back at him, erect, her face like a strained flag. "Why, of course," the druggist said. "If that's what you want. But the law requires you to tell what you are going to use it for."

Miss Emily just stared at him, her head tilted back in order to look him eye for eye, until he looked away and went and got the arsenic and wrapped it up. The Negro delivery boy brought her the package; the druggist didn't come back. When she opened the package at home there was written on the box, under the skull and bones: "For rats."

So the next day we all said, "She will kill herself"; and we said it would be the best thing. When she had first begun to be seen with Homer Barron, we had said, "She will marry him." Then we said, "She will persuade him yet," because Homer himself had remarked —he liked men, and it was known that he drank with the younger men in the Elks' Club —that he was not a marrying man. Later we said, "Poor Emily" behind the jalousies as they passed on Sunday afternoon in the glittering buggy, Miss Emily with her head high and Homer Barron with his hat cocked and a cigar in his teeth, reins and whip in a yellow glove.

Then some of the ladies began to say that it was a disgrace to the town and a bad example to the young people. The men did not want to interfere, but at last the ladies forced the Baptist minister—Miss Emily's people were Episcopal—to call upon her. He would never divulge what happened during that interview, but he refused to go back again. The next Sunday they again drove about the streets, and the following day the minister's wife wrote to Miss Emily's relations in Alabama.

So she had blood-kin under her roof again and we sat back to watch developments. At first nothing happened. Then we were sure that they were to be married. We learned that Miss Emily had been to the jeweler's and ordered a man's toilet set in silver, with the letters H. B. on each piece. Two days later we learned that she had bought a complete outfit of men's clothing, including a nightshirt, and we said, "They are married." We were really glad. We were glad because the two female cousins were even more Grierson than Miss Emily had ever been.

So we were not surprised when Homer Barron—the streets had been finished some time since—was gone. We were a little disappointed that there was not a public blowing-off, but we believed that he had gone on to prepare for Miss Emily's coming, or to give her a chance to get rid of the cousins. (By that time it was a cabal, and we were all Miss Emily's allies to help circumvent the cousins.) Sure enough, after another week they departed. And, as we had expected all along, within three days Homer Barron was back in town. A neighbor saw the Negro man admit him at the kitchen door at dusk one evening.

And that was the last we saw of Homer Barron. And of Miss Emily for some time. The Negro man went in and out with the market basket, but the front door remained closed. Now and then we would see her at a window for a moment, as the men did that night when they sprinkled the lime, but for almost six months she did not appear on the streets. Then we knew that this was to be expected too; as if that quality of her father which had thwarted her woman's life so many times had been too virulent and too furious to die.

When we next saw Miss Emily, she had grown fat and her hair was turning gray. During the next few years it grew grayer and grayer until it attained an even pepper-and-salt iron-gray, when it ceased turning. Up to the day of her death at seventy-four it was still that vigorous iron-gray, like the hair of an active man.

From that time on her front door remained closed, save for a period of six or seven years, when she was about forty, during which she gave lessons in china-painting. She fitted up a studio in one of the downstairs rooms, where the daughters and granddaughters of Colonel Sartoris' contemporaries were sent to her with the same regularity and in the same spirit that they were sent to church on Sundays with a twenty-five-cent piece for the collection plate. Meanwhile her taxes had been remitted.

Then the newer generation became the backbone and the spirit of the town, and the painting pupils grew up and fell away and did not send their children to her with boxes of color and tedious brushes and pictures cut from the ladies' magazines. The front door closed upon the last one and remained closed for good. When the town got free postal delivery, Miss Emily alone refused to let them fasten the metal numbers above her door and attach a mailbox to it. She would not listen to them.

Daily, monthly, yearly we watched the Negro grow grayer and more stooped, going in and out with the market basket. Each December we sent her a tax notice, which would be returned by the post office a week later, unclaimed. Now and then we would see her in one of the downstairs windows—she had evidently shut up the top floor of the house—like the carven torso of an idol in a niche, looking or not looking at us, we could never tell which. Thus she passed from generation to generation—dear, inescapable, impervious, tranquil, and perverse.

And so she died. Fell ill in the house filled with dust and shadows, with only a doddering Negro man to wait on her. We did not even know she was sick; we had long since given up trying to get any information from the Negro. He talked to no one, probably not even to her, for his voice had grown harsh and rusty, as if from disuse.

She died in one of the downstairs rooms, in a heavy walnut bed with a curtain, her gray head propped on a pillow yellow and moldy with age and lack of sunlight.

The Negro met the first of the ladies at the front door and let them in, with their hushed, sibilant voices and their quick, curious glances, and then he disappeared. He walked right through the house and out the back and was not seen again.

The two female cousins came at once. They held the funeral on the second day, with the town coming to look at Miss Emily beneath a mass of bought flowers, with the crayon face of her father musing profoundly above the bier and the ladies sibilant and macabre; and the very old men—some in their brushed Confederate uniforms—on the porch and the lawn, talking of Miss Emily as if she had been a contemporary of theirs, believing that they had danced with her and courted her perhaps, confusing time with its mathematical progression, as the old do, to whom all the past is not a diminishing road but, instead, a huge meadow which no winter ever quite touches, divided from them now by the narrow bottle-neck of the most recent decade of years.

Already we knew that there was one room in that region above stairs which no one had seen in forty years, and which would have to be forced. They waited until Miss Emily was decently in the ground before they opened it.

The violence of breaking down the door seemed to fill this room with pervading dust. A thin, acrid pall as of the tomb seemed to lie everywhere upon this room decked and furnished as for a bridal: upon the valance curtains of faded rose color, upon the rose-shaded lights, upon the dressing table, upon the delicate array of crystal and the man's toilet things backed with tarnished silver, silver so tarnished that the monogram was obscured. Among them lay a collar and tie, as if they had just been removed, which, lifted, left upon the surface a pale crescent in the dust. Upon a chair hung the suit, carefully folded; beneath it the two mute shoes and the discarded socks.

The man himself lay in the bed.

For a long while we just stood there, looking down at the profound and fleshless grin. The body had apparently once lain in the attitude of an embrace, but now the long sleep that outlasts love, that conquers even the grimace of love, had cuckolded him. What was left of him, rotted beneath what was left of the nightshirt, had become inextricable from the bed in which he lay; and upon him and upon the pillow beside him lay that even coating of the patient and biding dust.

Then we noticed that in the second pillow was the indentation of a head. One of us lifted something from it, and leaning forward, that faint and invisible dust dry and acrid in the nostrils, we saw a long strand of iron-gray hair.

Story 4

"The Appointment in Samarra"

(as retold by W. Somerset Maugham [1933])

The speaker is Death

There was a merchant in Bagdad who sent his servant to market to buy provisions and in a little while the servant came back, white and trembling, and said, Master, just now when I was in the marketplace I was jostled by a woman in the crowd and when I turned I saw it was Death that jostled me. She looked at me and made a threatening gesture, now, lend me your horse, and I will ride away from this city and avoid my fate. I will go to Samarra and there Death will not find me. The merchant lent him his horse, and the servant mounted it, and he dug his spurs in its flanks and as fast as the horse could gallop he went. Then the merchant went down to the marketplace and he saw me standing in the crowd and he came to me and said, Why did you make a threating getsture to my servant when you saw him this morning? That was not a threatening gesture, I said, it was only a start of surprise. I was astonished to see him in Bagdad, for I had an appointment with him tonight in Samarra.

Story 5

The Facts Concerning the Recent Carnival of Crime in Connecticut by Mark Twain

I said to myself, 'I am thoroughly happy and content, now. If my most pitiless enemy could appear before me at this moment, I would freely right any wrong I may have done him'"

I was feeling blithe, almost jocund. I put a match to my cigar, and just then the morning's mail was handed in. The first superscription I glanced at was in a handwriting that sent a thrill of pleasure through and through me. It was aunt Mary's; and she was the person I loved and honored most in all the world, outside of my own household. She had been my boyhood's idol; maturity, which is fatal to so many enchantments, had not been able to dislodge her from her pedestal; no, it had only justified her right to be there, and placed her dethronement permanently among the impossibilities. To show how strong her influence over me was, I will observe that long after everybody else's "*do*-stop-smoking" had ceased to affect me in the slightest degree, aunt Mary could still stir my torpid conscience into faint signs of life when she touched upon the matter. But all things have their limit, in this world. A happy day came at last, when even aunt Mary's words could no longer move me. I was not merely glad to see that day arrive; I was more than glad—I was grateful; for when its sun had set, the one alloy that was able to mar my enjoyment of my aunt's society was gone. The remainder of her stay with us that winter was in every way a delight. Of course she pleaded with me just as earnestly as ever, after that blessed day, to quit my pernicious habit, but to no purpose whatever; the moment she opened the subject I at once became calmly, peacefully, contentedly indifferent—absolutely, adamantinely indifferent. Consequently the closing weeks of that memorable visit melted away as pleasantly as a dream, they were so freighted, for me, with tranquil satisfaction. I could not have enjoyed my pet vice more if my gentle tormentor had been a smoker herself, and an advocate of the practice. Well, the sight of her handwriting reminded me that I was getting very hungry to see her again. I easily guessed what I should find in her letter. I opened it. Good! just as I expected; she was coming! Coming this very day, too, and by the morning train; I might expect her any moment.

I said to myself, "I am thoroughly happy and content, now. If my most pitiless enemy could appear before me at this moment, I would freely right any wrong I may have done him."

Straightway the door opened, and a shriveled, shabby dwarf entered. He was not more than two feet high. He seemed to be about forty years old. Every feature and every inch of him was a trifle out of shape; and so, while one could not put his finger upon any particular part and say, "This is a conspicuous deformity," the spectator perceived that this little person was a deformity as a whole—a vague, general, evenly-blended, nicely-adjusted deformity. There was a fox-like cunning, in the face and the sharp little eyes, and also alertness and malice. And yet, this vile bit of human rubbish seemed to bear a sort of remote and ill-defined resemblance to me! It was dully perceptible in the mean form, the countenance, and even the clothes, gestures, manner, and attitudes of the creature. He was a far-fetched, dim suggestion of a burlesque upon me, a caricature of me in little. One thing about him struck me forcibly, and most unpleasantly: he was covered all over with a fuzzy, greenish mold, such as one sometimes sees upon mildewed bread. The sight of it was nauseating.

He stepped along with a chipper air, and flung himself into a doll's chair in a very free and easy way, without waiting to be asked. He tossed his hat into the waste basket. He picked up my old chalk pipe from the floor, gave the stem a wipe or two on his knee, filled the bowl from the tobacco-box at his side, and said to me in a tone of pert command, —

"Gimme a match!"

I blushed to the roots of my hair; partly with indignation, but mainly because it somehow seemed to me that this whole performance was very like an exaggeration of conduct which I myself had sometimes been guilty of in my intercourse with familiar friends,— but never, never with strangers, I observed to myself. I wanted to kick the pygmy into the fire, but some incomprehensible sense of being legally and legitimately under his authority forced me to obey his order. He applied the match to the pipe, took a contemplative whiff or two, and remarked, in an irritatingly familiar way, —

"Seems to me it 's devilish odd weather for this time of year."

I flushed again, and in anger and humiliation as before; for the language was hardly an exaggeration of some that I have uttered in my day, and moreover was delivered in a tone of voice and with an exasperating drawl that had the seeming of a deliberate travesty of my style. Now there is nothing I am quite so sensitive about as a mocking imitation of my drawling infirmity of speech. I spoke up sharply and said,—

"Look here, you miserable ash-cat! you will have to give a little more attention to your manners, or I will throw you out of the window!"

The manikin smiled a smile of malicious content and security, puffed a whiff of smoke contemptuously toward me, and said, with a still more elaborate drawl,—

"Come—go gently, now; don't put on *too* many airs with your betters."

This cool snub rasped me all over, but it seemed to subjugate me, too, for a moment. The pygmy contemplated me a while with his weasel eyes, and then said, in a peculiarly sneering way,—

"You turned a tramp away from your door this morning."

I said crustily, —

"Perhaps I did, perhaps I did n't. How do *you* know?"

"Well, I know. It is n't any matter *how* I know."

"Very well. Suppose I *did* turn a tramp away from the door—what of it?"

"Oh, nothing; nothing in particular. Only you lied to him."

"I *did* n't! That is, I"—

"Yes, but you did; you lied to him."

I felt a guilty pang,—in truth I had felt it forty times before that tramp had traveled a block from my door,—but still I resolved to make a show of feeling slandered; so I said, —

"This is a baseless impertinence. I said to the tramp"—

"There—wait. You were about to lie again. *I* know what you said to him. You said the cook was gone down to town and there was nothing left from breakfast. Two lies. You knew the cook was behind the door, and plenty of provisions behind *her*."

This astonishing accuracy silenced me; and it filled me with wondering speculations, too, as to how this cub could have got his information. Of course he could have culled the conversation from the tramp, but by what sort of magic had he contrived to find out about the concealed cook? Now the dwarf spoke again:—

"It was rather pitiful, rather small, in you to refuse to read that poor young woman's manuscript the other day, and give her an opinion as to its literary value; and she had come so far, too, and *so* hopefully. Now *was n't* it?"

I felt like a cur! And I had felt so every time the thing had recurred to my mind, I may as well confess. I flushed hotly and said,—

"Look here, have you nothing better to do than prowl around prying into other people's business? Did that girl tell you that?"

"Never mind whether she did or not. The main thing is, you did that contemptible thing. And you felt ashamed of it afterwards. Aha! you feel ashamed of it *now!*"

This with a sort of devilish glee. With fiery earnestness I responded,—

"I told that girl, in the kindest, gentlest way, that I could not consent to deliver judgment upon *any* one's manuscript, because an individual's verdict was worthless. It might underrate a work of high merit and lose it to the world, or it might overrate a trashy production and so open the way for its infliction upon the world. I said that the great public was the only tribunal competent to sit in judgment upon a literary effort, and therefore it must be best to lay it before that tribunal in the outset, since in the end it must stand or fall by that mighty court's decision any way."

"Yes, you said all that. So you did, you juggling, small-souled shuffler! And yet when the happy hopefulness faded out of that poor girl's face, when you saw her furtively slip beneath her shawl the scroll she had so patiently and honestly scribbled at,—so ashamed of her darling now, so proud of it before,—when you saw the gladness go out of her eyes and the tears come there, when she crept away so humbly who had come so"—

"Oh, peace! peace! peace! Blister your merciless tongue, have n't all these thoughts tortured me enough, without *your* coming here to fetch them back again?"

Remorse! remorse! It seemed to me that it would eat the very heart out of me! And yet that small fiend only sat there leering at me with joy and contempt, and placidly chuckling. Presently he began to speak again. Every sentence was an accusation, and every accusation a truth. Every clause was freighted with sarcasm and derision, ever slow-dropping word burned like vitriol. The dwarf reminded me of times when I had flown at my children in anger and punished them for faults which a little inquiry would have taught me that others, and not they, had committed. He reminded me of how I had disloyally allowed old friends to be traduced in my hearing, and been too craven to utter a word in their defense. He reminded me of many dishonest things which I had done; of many which I had procured to be done by children and other irresponsible persons; of some which I had planned, thought upon, and longed to do, and been kept from the performance by fear of consequences only. With exquisite cruelty he recalled to my mind, item by item, wrongs and unkindnesses I had inflicted and humiliations I had put upon friends since dead, "who died thinking of those injuries, maybe, and grieving, over them," he added, by way of poison to the stab.

"For instance," said he, "take the case of your younger brother, when you two were boys together, many a long year ago. He always lovingly trusted in you with a fidelity that your manifold treacheries were not able to shake. He followed you about like a dog, content to suffer wrong and abuse if he might only be with you; patient under these injuries so long as it was your hand that inflicted them. The latest picture you have of him in health and strength must be such a comfort to you! You pledged your honor that if he would let you blindfold him no harm should come to him; and then, giggling and choking over the rare fun of the joke, you led him to a brook thinly glazed with ice, and pushed him in; and how you did laugh! Man, you will never forget the gentle, reproachful look he gave you as he struggled shivering out, if you live a thousand years! Oho! you see it now, you see it *now*! "

"Beast, I have seen it a million times, and shall see it a million more! and may you rot away piecemeal, and suffer till doomsday what I suffer now, for bringing it back to me again!"

The dwarf chuckled contentedly, and went on with his accusing history of my career. I dropped into a moody, vengeful state, and suffered in silence under the merciless lash. At last this remark of his grave gave me a sudden rouse: —

"Two months ago, on a Tuesday, you woke up, away in the night, and fell to thinking, with shame, about a peculiarly mean and pitiful act of yours toward a poor ignorant Indian in the wilds of the Rocky Mountains in the winter of eighteen hundred and" —

"Stop a moment, devil! Stop! Do you mean to tell me that even my very thoughts are not hidden from you?"

"It seems to look like that. Did n't you think the thoughts I have just mentioned?"

"If I did n't, I wish I may never breathe again! Look here, friend—look me in the eye. Who *are* you?

"Well, who do you think?"

"I think you are Satan himself. I think you are the devil."

"No."

"No? Then who *can* you be?"

"Would you really like to know?"

"*Indeed* I would."

"Well, I am your *Conscience*!"

In an instant I was in a blaze of joy and exultation. I sprang at the creature, roaring,—

"Curse you, I have wished a hundred million times that you were tangible, and that I could get my hands on your throat once! Oh, but I will wreak deadly vengeance on"—

Folly! Lightning does not move more quickly than my Conscience did! He darted aloft so suddenly that in the moment my fingers clutched the empty air he was already perched on the top of the high book-case, with his thumb at his nose in token of derision. I flung the poker at him, and missed. I fired the boot-jack. In a blind rage I flew from place to place, and snatched and hurled any missile that came handy; the storm of books, inkstands, and chunks of coal gloomed the air and beat about the manikin's perch relentlessly, but all to no purpose; the nimble figure dodged every shot; and not only that, but burst into a cackle of sarcastic and triumphant laughter as I sat down exhausted. While I puffed and gasped with fatigue and excitement, my Conscience talked to this effect:—

"My good slave, you are curiously witless—no, I mean characteristically so. In truth, you are always consistent, always yourself, always an ass. Otherwise it must have occurred to you that if you attempted this murder with a sad heart and a heavy conscience, I would droop under the burdening influence instantly. Fool, I should have weighed a ton, and could not have budged from the floor; but instead, you are so cheerfully anxious to kill me that your conscience is as light as a feather; hence I am away up here out of your reach. I can almost respect a mere ordinary sort of fool; but *you*—pah!"

I would have given anything, then, to be heavy-hearted, so that I could get this person down from there and take his life but I could no more be heavy-hearted over such a desire than I could have sorrowed over its accomplishment. So I could only look longingly up at my master, and rave at the ill-luck that denied me a heavy conscience the one only time that I had ever wanted such a thing in my life. By and by I got to musing over the hour's strange adventure, and of course my human curiosity began to work. I set myself to framing in my mind some questions for this fiend to answer. Just then one of my boys entered, leaving the door open behind him, and exclaimed,—

"My! what *has* been going on, here! The book-case is all one riddle of" —

I sprang up in consternation, and shouted, —

"Out of this! Hurry! Jump! Fly! Shut the door! Quick, or my Conscience will get away!"

The door slammed to, and I locked it, I glanced up and was grateful, to the bottom of my heart, to see that my owner was still my prisoner. I said, —

"Hang you, I might have lost you! Children are the heedlessest creatures. But look here, friend, the boy did not seem to notice you at all; how is that?"

"For a very good reason. I am invisible to all but you."

I made mental note of that piece of information with a good deal of satisfaction. I could kill this miscreant now, if I got a chance, and no one would know it. But this very reflection made me so light-hearted that my Conscience could hardly keep his seat, but was like to float aloft toward the ceiling like a toy balloon. I said, presently, —

"Come, my Conscience, let us be friendly. Let us fly a flag of truce for a while. I am suffering to ask you some questions."

"Very well. Begin."

"Well, then, in the first place, why were you never visible to me before?"

"Because you never asked to see me before; that is, you never asked in the right spirit and the proper form before. You were just in the right spirit this time, and when you called for your most pitiless enemy I was that person by a very large majority, though you did not suspect it."

"Well, did that remark of mine turn you into flesh and blood?"

"No. It only made me visible to you. I am unsubstantial, just as other spirits are."

This remark prodded me with a sharp misgiving. If he was unsubstantial, how was I going to kill him? But I dissembled, and said persuasively, —

"Conscience, it is n't sociable of you to keep at such a distance. Come down and take another smoke."

This was answered with a look that was full of derision, and with this observation added: —

"Come where you can get at me and kill me? The invitation is declined with thanks."

"All right," said I to myself; "so it seems a spirit *can* be killed, after all; there will be one spirit lacking in this world, presently, or I lose my guess." Then I said aloud, —

"Friend" —

"There; wait a bit. I am not your friend, I am your enemy; I am not your equal, I am your master. Call me 'my lord,' if you please. You are too familiar."

"I don't like such titles. I am willing to call you *sir*. That is as far as" —

"We will have no argument about this. Just obey; that is all. Go on with your chatter."

"Very well, my lord,—since nothing but my lord will suit you,—I was going to ask you how long you will be visible to me?"

"Always!"

I broke out with strong indignation: "This is simply an outrage. That is what I think of it. You have dogged, and dogged, and *dogged* me, all the days of my life, invisible. That was misery enough; now to have such a sorry looking thing as you tagging after me like another shadow all the rest of my days is an intolerable prospect. You have my opinion, my lord; make the most of it."

"My lad, there was never so pleased a conscience in this world as I was when you made me visible. It gives me an inconceivable advantage. *Now,* I can look you straight in the eye, and call you names, and leer at you, jeer at you, sneer at you; and *you* know what eloquence there is in visible gesture and expression, more especially when the effect is heightened by audible speech. I shall always address you henceforth in your o-w-n s-n-i-v-e-l-i-n-g d-r-a-w-l—baby!"

I let fly with the coal-hod. No result. My lord said,—

"Come, come! Remember the flag of truce!"

"Ah, I forgot that. I will try to be civil; and you try it, too, for a novelty. The idea of a *civil* conscience! It is a good joke; an excellent joke. All the consciences I have ever heard of were nagging, badgering, fault-finding execrable savages! Yes; and always in a sweat about some poor little insignificant trifle or other—destruction catch the lot of them, I say! I would trade mine for the smallpox and seven kinds of consumption, and be glad of the chance. Now tell me, why *is* it that a conscience can't haul a man over the coals once, for an offense, and then let him alone? Why is it that it wants to keep on pegging at him, day and night and night and day, week in and week out, forever and ever, about the same old thing? There is no sense in that, and no reason in it. I think a conscience that will act like that is meaner than the very dirt itself."

"Well, *we* like it; that suffices."

"Do you do it with the honest intent to improve a man?"

That question produced a sarcastic smile, and this reply: —

"No, sir. Excuse me. We do it simply because it is 'business.' It is our trade. The *purpose* of it *is* to improve the man, but we are merely disinterested agents. We are appointed by authority, and have n't anything to say in the matter. We obey orders and leave the consequences where they belong. But I am willing to admit this much: we *do* crowd the orders a trifle when we get a chance, which is most of the time. We enjoy it. We are instructed to remind a man a few times of an error; and I don't mind acknowledging that we try to give pretty good measure. And when we get hold of a man of a peculiarly sensitive nature, oh, but we do haze him! I have known consciences to come all the way from China and Russia to see a person of that kind put through his paces, on a special occasion. Why, I knew a man of that sort who had accidentally crippled a mulatto baby; the news went abroad, and I wish you may never commit another sin if the consciences did n' t flock from all over the earth to enjoy the fun and help his master exercise him. That man walked the floor in torture for forty-eight hours, without eating or sleeping, and then blew his brains out. The child was perfectly well again in three weeks."

"Well, you are a precious crew, not to put it too strong. I think I begin to see, now, why you have always been a trifle inconsistent with me. In your anxiety to get all the juice you can out of a sin, you make a man repent of it in three or four different ways. For instance, you found fault with me for lying to that tramp, and I suffered over that. But it was only yesterday that I told a tramp the square truth, to wit, that, it being regarded as bad citizenship to encourage vagrancy, I would give him nothing. What did you do *then*? Why, you made me say to myself, 'Ah, it would have been so much kinder and more blameless to ease him off with a little white lie, and send him away feeling that if he could not have bread, the gentle treatment was at least something to be grateful for!' Well, I suffered all day about *that*. Three days before, I had fed a tramp, and fed him freely, supposing it a virtuous act. Straight off you said, 'O false citizen, to have fed a tramp!' and I suffered as usual. I gave a tramp work; you objected to it, — *after* the contract was made, of course; you never speak up beforehand. Next, I *refused* a tramp work; you objected to *that*. Next, I proposed to kill a tramp; you kept me awake all night, oozing remorse at every pore. Sure I was going to be right *this* time, I sent the next tramp away with my benediction; and I wish you may live as long as I do, if you did n't make me smart all night again because I did n't kill him. Is there *any* way of satisfying that malignant invention which is called a Conscience?"

"Ha, ha! this is luxury! Go on!"

"But come, now, answer me that question. *Is* there any way?"

"Well, none that I propose to tell *you*, my son. Ass! I don't care *what* act you may turn your hand to, I can straightway whisper a word in your ear and make you think you have committed a dreadful meanness. It is my *business* — and my joy — to make you repent of *every*thing you do. If I have fooled away any opportunities it was not intentional; I beg to assure you it was not intentional."

"Don't worry; you haven't missed a trick that *I* know of. I never did a thing in all my life, virtuous or otherwise, that I did n't repent of within twenty-four hours. In church last Sunday I listened to a charity sermon. My first impulse was to give three hundred and fifty dollars; I repented of that and reduced it another hundred; repented of that, and reduced it another hundred; repented of that and reduced it another hundred; repented of that and reduced the remaining fifty to twenty-five; repented of that and came down to fifteen; repented of that and dropped to two dollars and a half; when the plate came around at last, I repented once more and contributed ten cents. Well, when I got home, I did wish to goodness I had that ten cents back again! You never *did* let me get through a charity sermon without having something to sweat about."

"Oh, and I never shall, I never shall. You can always depend on me."

"I think so. Many and many's the restless night I've wanted to take you by the neck. If I could only get hold of you now!"

"Yes, no doubt. But I am not an ass; I am only the saddle of an ass. But go on, go on. You entertain me more than I like to confess."

"I am glad of that. (You will not mind my lying a little, to keep in practice.) Look here; not to be too personal, I think you are about the shabbiest and most contemptible little shriveled-up reptile that can be imagined. I am grateful enough that you are invisible to other people, for I should die with shame to be seen with such a mildewed monkey of a conscience as *you* are. Now if you were five or six feet high, and" —

"Oh, come! who is to blame?"

"*I* don't know."

"Why, you are; nobody else."

"Confound you, I was n't consulted about your personal appearance."

"I don't care, you had a good deal to do with it, nevertheless. When you were eight or nine years old, I was seven feet high and as pretty as a picture."

"I wish you had died young! So you have grown the wrong way, have you?"

"Some of us grow one way and some the other. You had a large conscience once; if you 've a small conscience now, I reckon there are reasons for it. However, both of us are to blame, you and I. You see, you used to be conscientious about a great many things; morbidly so, I may say. It was a great many years ago. You probably do not remember it, now. Well, I took a great interest in my work, and I so enjoyed the anguish which certain pet sins of yours afflicted you with, that I kept pelting at you until I rather overdid the matter. You began to rebel. Of course I began to lose ground, then, and shrivel a little, — diminish in stature, get moldy, and grow deformed. The more I weakened, the more stubbornly you fastened on to those particular sins; till at last the places on my person that represent those vices became as callous as shark skin. Take smoking, for instance. I played that card a little too long, and I lost. When people plead with you at this late day to quit that vice, that old callous place seems to enlarge and cover me all over like a shirt of mail. It exerts a mysterious, smothering, effect; and presently I, your faithful hater, your devoted Conscience, go sound asleep! Sound? It is no name for it. I could n't hear it thunder at such a time. You have some few other vices—perhaps eighty, or maybe ninety —that affect me in much the same way."

"This is flattering; you must be asleep a good part of your time."

"Yes, of late years. I should be asleep *all* the time, but for the help I get."

"Who helps you?"

"Other consciences. Whenever a person whose conscience I am acquainted with tries to plead with you about the vices you are callous to, I get my friend to give his client a pang, concerning some villainy of his own, and that shuts off his meddling and starts him off to hunt personal consolation. My field of usefulness is about trimmed down to tramps, budding authoresses, and that line of goods, now; but don't you worry—I'll harry you on *them* while they last! Just you put your trust in me."

"I think I can. But if you had only been good enough to mention these facts some thirty years ago, I should have turned my particular attention to sin, and I think that by this time I should not only have had you pretty permanently asleep on the entire list of human vices, but reduced to the size of a homeopathic pill, at that. That is about the style of conscience *I* am pining for. If I only had you shrunk down to a homeopathic pill, and could get my hands on you, would I put you in a glass case for a keepsake? No, sir. I would give you to a yellow dog! That is where *you* ought to be—you and all your tribe. You are not fit to be in society, in my opinion. Now another question. Do you know a good many consciences in this section?"

"Plenty of them."

"I would give anything to see some of them! Could you bring them here? And would they be visible to me?"

"Certainly not."

"I suppose I ought to have known that, without asking. But no matter, you can describe them. Tell me about my neighbor Thompson's conscience, please."

"Very well. I know him intimately; have known him many years. I knew him when he was eleven feet high and of a faultless figure. But he is very rusty and tough and misshapen, now, and hardly ever interests himself about anything. As to his present size —well, he sleeps in a cigar box."

"Likely enough. There are few smaller, meaner men in this region than Hugh Thompson. Do you know Robinson's conscience?"

"Yes. He is a shade under four and a half feet high; used to be a blonde; is a brunette, now, but still shapely and comely." "Well, Robinson is a good fellow. Do you know Tom Smith's conscience?"

"I have known him from childhood. He was thirteen inches high, and rather sluggish, when he was two years old—as nearly all of us are, at that age. He is thirty-seven feet high, now, and the stateliest figure in America. His legs are still racked with growing-pains, but he has a good time, nevertheless. Never sleeps. He is the most active and energetic member of the New England Conscience Club; is president of it. Night and day you can find him pegging away at Smith, panting with his labor, sleeves rolled up, countenance all alive with enjoyment. He has got his victim splendidly dragooned, now. He can make poor Smith imagine that the most innocent little thing he does is an odious sin; and then he sets to work and almost tortures the soul out of him about it."

"Smith is the noblest man in all this section, and the purest; and yet is always breaking his heart because he cannot be good! Only a conscience *could* find pleasure in helping agony upon a spirit like that. Do you know my aunt Mary's conscience?"

"I have seen her at a distance, but am not acquainted with her. She lives in the open air altogether, because no door is large enough to admit her."

"I can believe that. Let me see. Do you know the conscience of that publisher who once stole some sketches of mine for a 'series' of his, and then left me to pay the law expenses I had to incur in order to choke him off?"

"Yes. He has a wide fame. He was exhibited, a month ago, with some other antiquities, for the benefit of a recent Member of the Cabinet's conscience that was starving in exile. Tickets and fares were high, but I traveled for nothing by pretending to be the conscience of an editor, and get in for half price by representing myself to be the conscience of a clergyman. However, the publisher's conscience, which was to have been the main feature of the entertainment, was a failure—as an exhibition. He was there, but what of that? The management had provided a microscope with a magnifying power of only thirty thousand diameters, and so nobody got to see him, after all. There was great and general dissatisfaction, of course, but"—

Just here there was an eager footstep on the stair; I opened the door, and my aunt Mary burst into the room. It was a joyful meeting, and a cheery bombardment of questions and answers concerning family matters ensued. By and by my aunt said,—

"But I am going to abuse you a little now. You promised me, the day I saw you last, that you would look after the needs of the poor family around the corner as faithfully as I had done it myself. Well, I found out by accident that you failed of your promise. *Was* that right ?"

In simple truth, I never had thought of that family a second time! And now such a splintering pang of guilt shot through me! I glanced up at my Conscience. Plainly, my heavy heart was affecting him. His body was drooping forward; he seemed about to fall from the bookcase. My aunt continued: —

And think how you have neglected my poor *protégée* at the almshouse, you dear, hard-hearted promise-breaker!" I blushed scarlet, and my tongue was tied. As the sense of my guilty negligence waxed sharper and stronger, my Conscience begin to sway heavily back and forth; and when my aunt, after a little pause, said in a grieved tone, "Since you never once went to see her, maybe it will not distress you now to know that that poor child died, months ago, utterly friendless and forsaken!" my Conscience could no longer bear up under the weight of my sufferings, but tumbled headlong from his high perch and struck the floor with a dull, leaden thump. He lay there writhing with pain and quaking with apprehension, but straining, every muscle in frantic efforts to get up. In a fever of expectancy I sprang to the door, locked it, placed my back against it, and bent a watchful gaze upon my struggling master. Already my fingers were itching to began their murderous work. "Oh, what can be the matter!" exclaimed my aunt, shrinking from me, and following with her frightened eyes the direction off mine. My breath was coming, in short, quick gasps now, and my excitement was almost uncontrollable. My aunt cried out, —

"Oh, do not look so! You appall me! Oh, what can the matter be? What is it you see? Why do you stare so? Why do you work your fingers like that?"

"Peace, woman!" I said, in a hoarse whisper. "Look elsewhere; pay no attention to me; it is nothing—nothing. I am often this way. It will pass in a moment. It comes from smoking too much."

My injured lord was up, wild-eyed with terror, and trying to hobble toward the door. I could hardly breathe, I was so wrought up. My aunt wrung her hands, and said, —

"Oh, I knew how it would be; I knew it would come to this at last! Oh, I implore you to crush out that fatal habit while it may yet be time! You must not, you shall not be deaf to my supplications longer!" My struggling Conscience showed sudden signs of weariness! "Oh, promise me you will throw off this hateful slavery of tobacco!" My Conscience began to reel drowsily, and grope with his hands—enchanting spectacle! "I beg you, I beseech you, I implore you! Your reason is deserting you! There is madness in your eye! It flames with frenzy! Oh, hear me, hear me, and be saved! See, I plead with you on my very knees!" As she sank before me my Conscience reeled again, and then drooped languidly to the floor, blinking toward me a last supplication for mercy, with heavy eyes.

"Oh, promise, or you are lost! Promise, and be redeemed! Promise! Promise and live!" With a long-drawn sigh my conquered Conscience closed his eyes and fell fast asleep!

With an exultant shout I sprang past my aunt, and in an instant I had my life-long foe by the throat. After so many years of waiting and longing, he was mine at last. I tore him to shreds and fragments. I rent the fragments to bits. I cast the bleeding rubbish into the fire, and drew into my nostrils the grateful incense of my burnt-offering. At last, and forever, my Conscience was dead!

I was a free man! I turned upon my poor aunt, who was almost petrified with terror, and shouted,—

"Out of this with your paupers, your charities, your reforms, your pestilent morals! You behold before you a man whose life-conflict is done, whose soul is at peace; a man whose heart is dead to sorrow, dead to suffering, dead to remorse; a man WITHOUT A CONSCIENCE! In my joy I spare you, though I could throttle you and never feel a pang! Fly!"

She fled. Since that day my life is all bliss. Bliss, unalloyed bliss. Nothing in all the world could persuade me to have a conscience again. I settled all my old outstanding scores, and began the world anew. I killed thirty-eight persons during the first two weeks— all of them on account of ancient grudges. I burned a dwelling that interrupted my view. I swindled a widow and some orphans out of their last cow, which is a very good one, though not thoroughbred, I believe. I have also committed scores of crimes, of various kinds, and have enjoyed my work exceedingly, whereas it would formerly have broken my heart and turned my hair gray, I have no doubt.

In conclusion I wish to state, by way of advertisement, that medical colleges desiring assorted tramps for scientific purposes, either by the gross, by cord measurement, or per ton, will do well to examine the lot in my cellar before purchasing elsewhere, as these were all selected and prepared by myself, and can be had at a low rate, because I wish to clear out my stock and get ready for the spring trade.

PRACTICE STEP FOUR - SUMMARIZING AND PARAPHRASING ACTIVITY

Now that you've decided on the order of the news stories please go about re-writing each short story into a news story (like you are writing it for a newspaper) complete with a headline. Each story (because they are of different emphasis) will be of different length.

Story 1 1000 words (front page, most important story)
Story 2 800 words
Story 3 600 words
Story 4 400 words
Story 5 200 words (back page, least important story)

This is about the order that you chose in your group NOT about the original order of the stories listed above.

Each group member will just be responsible for writing a news story based on their reading. One person will collect each submission from the group and then format it into a newsletter (or use a newspaper template to make it look like a newspaper).

IF YOU HAVE SIX MEMBERS IN YOUR GROUP THERE IS A SPECIAL EXTRA TASK
The sixth member will be the EDITOR. The EDITOR will write a short paragraph commenting on each of the final news stories and why each was chosen to be in the position it is (first, second. . .).

The role of paraphrasing and summarizing:

A summary of the events condenses the details of the story into a form suitable for the attention span of a newspaper.

Paraphrasing clarifies the issues of the story. If someone dies under mysterious circumstances (or implied circumstances) in the story, you might want to clarify this point in your newspaper article.

Made in the USA
Lexington, KY
06 August 2012